Pete's
mailbag

GARDENING AUSTRALIA

ABC
BOOKS

Pete's mailbag

Original tips and ideas from Australian gardeners

Disclaimer

All these hints and tips have been published in good faith and no responsibility will be taken for their effectiveness. Like all gardening, it is a matter of trial and error.

Published by ABC Books for the
AUSTRALIAN BROADCASTING CORPORATION
GPO Box 9994 Sydney NSW 2001

First published 2001
Reprinted October 2001
Reprinted May 2002

National Library of Australia
Cataloguing-in-Publication entry
Pete's mailbag: original tips and ideas from Australian gardeners.
Includes index.
ISBN 0 7333 1048 6.
1. Gardening – Australia. 2. Gardening – Australia – Equipment and supplies. I. Cundall, Peter, 1927– .
II. Australian Broadcasting Corporation. III. Title.
Gardening Australia (Television program).
635.0994

Illustrations by Steve Hilliard
Set in 12 pt Gill Sans
Colour separations by Colorwize, Adelaide
Printed and bound in Australia MPG

5 4 3

Welcome to Pete's mailbag

I'm never astonished by the cleverness of dedicated gardeners. Invention is the name of the game in the garden. We do it all the time. Faced with a problem, we immediately work out some kind of a solution. That's why every garden is filled with all sorts of simple or complex gadgets. They range from methods of securing or tying plants, to sophisticated, homemade greenhouses.

That's why we at *Gardening Australia* decided to tap the wisdom and experience of our gardening friends. We started *Pete's Mailbag*—on the television show and in the magazine—and a great flood of letters and funny-shaped packages poured in.

They came from the most remote parts of Australia and were crammed with ideas, suggestions, experiments, drawings, bits of rope, wire and, of course, plastic bottles of every shape and size.

There were far too many to be shown and demonstrated on *Gardening Australia*, and we don't believe in waste.

So here's the book. And that's *your* bloomin' lot!

Peter Cundall

PS Don't miss the handy subject index at the back of the book.

Bed & barrow

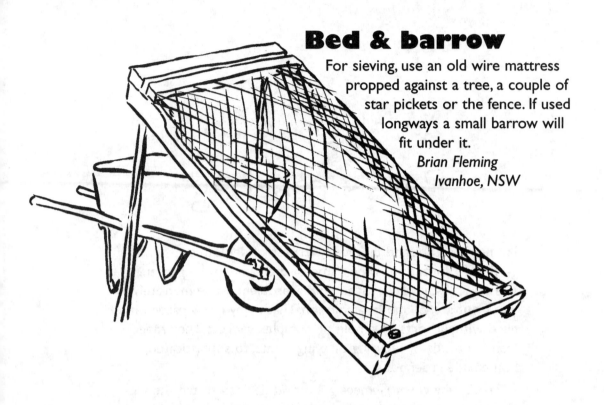

For sieving, use an old wire mattress propped against a tree, a couple of star pickets or the fence. If used longways a small barrow will fit under it.

Brian Fleming
Ivanhoe, NSW

The ultimate compost mixer

To make compost, take three buckets of cut grass, one of sandy soil and one of pulverised cow manure. Mix in cement mixer. Blood and bone can be added. Tip into a compost bin and sprinkle lightly with water. The result is very crumbly compost.

A B Logan, Cheltenham, NSW

Keeping track

Car or light truck tyres stacked on top of each other make an ideal container for compostable material. Five or six tyres can be used per container. A series of stacks enables appropriate conditioning or 'cooking' to take place. The advantages of this are that it requires no skill to make, it's non-destructable, easy to dismantle and reassemble, dog proof and eco-friendly.
Lindsay Moulden
Coffs Harbour, NSW

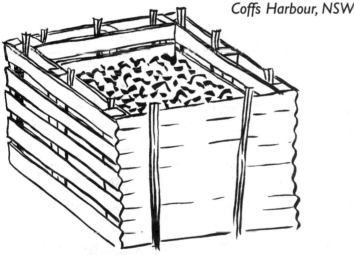

Palette power

Make a large compost bin using discarded palettes. Nail a few extra horizontal strips or use wire netting if the spaces are too wide. Hold using star posts hammered down inside. Use a piece of sheet roofing as a sliding opening.
Elaine Atkinson, Basin View, NSW

Wet it

For potting soil that does not absorb water in pots or the garden, use two drops of detergent to one litre of water. The result is instantaneous and only one treatment is needed.
J Chapman, Kerang, Vic

Lime limits

You often need to prepare the ground for adding lime but time between sowings may be against you. Don't wait for the lime, go ahead and plant. Then once a month water the plants with a solution of one tablespoon of lime to a watering can of water.
Allon Hofmoun, Toowoomba, Qld

Compost zapper

We had a compost heap that was too cool to kill seeds, so we were always getting a crop of little things in the flowerpots. We solved the problem by cutting off the seed heads into a supermarket bag, loosely tying it and popping it in the microwave for four minutes on high. Then they can be placed safely in the compost without propagating.

Jenny Anderson, Research, Vic

Instant compost

A recipe for instant compost, or rather instant food for compost makers—worms: Take a kitchen blender and half fill it with water. Add any vegetable peelings, dead house flowers, garden deadheads. Blend to consistency of vegetable soup. Spread the mixture directly onto the garden and cover lightly with soil. Leave the rest to the worms, they will have dealt with the food by the morning. The advantages are no smell, no flies, no mess, no turning compost.

Ivy Kenneady, White Cliffs, NSW

Seagrass recycling

Cut old squares of seagrass matting diagonally to the middle. Place each one with the cut edges around plants such as tomatoes. It provides good protection and later good mulch.

Chris Field, Auburn, Tas

Hanging out to dry

For a quick and efficient technique to dry out compost build a framework of approx 1x2m with two beams to support loosely laid 10mm-gauge shadecloth mesh. This framework is mounted on two house bricks at each corner, thus creating a through-draft cavity of approx. 20cm above the ground. It drags out all the moisture generated by the heat from the covering compost materials, thus eliminating the black sludge that is common with other types of compost. The compost is loosely compiled into pyramid-shaped rows as high as can be comfortably assembled, then covered with bags to retain rising heat. This process separates the sweating moisture from the compost, which will gradually work its way down and out of the compost. The end result is a thoroughly dried-out and brittle compost waste within four weeks.

Owen Cramp, Port Fairy, Vic

Seedling hats

To protect young, newly planted seedlings, use the plastic 'hat' from the top half of a two-litre juice container. It retains warmth from the sun and minimises moisture loss while also giving protection from the wind. It can be removed in a week or two when the seedling fills the available space.
Ian Lucas
Killara, NSW

Calcium boost

Save eggshells in a large jar after washing them Put them in the coffee grinder and make them into a powder. Sprinkle it over the vegie patch. This is full of calcium which the vegies can enjoy!
Athena Marini
Brunswick West, Vic

Tinsel tamers

Having problems with birds eating all the fruit on your trees? Don't pack away those long lengths of tinsel off the tree once Christmas is over, use them as a bird deterrent. They become quite disturbed by this bright, shiny alien hanging in the trees. The tinsel on wire is very useful as you can mould it around bunches. When sowing a new lawn criss-cross lengths of string all over the area about 10cm off the ground and tie lengths of silver gift tie periodically to keep the birds at bay.

Margaret Ryan, Horsham, Vic

Snake charmer

To get birds out of your garden, simply buy a plastic snake from a toy shop and place it where the bird roosts or near the nest. The birds will immediately desert the site and keep away long after you have removed the snake. But never use the snake charm when there are eggs or chicks in the nest as it would spell doom for them!

H Sydney Curtis, Hawthorne, Qld

The long reach

This is a home-made gardening aid for cutting down anything that's out of reach—from lemons to proteas. It is made out of an old broom handle, a short piece of fencing wire and two hose clips.

Hazel & Tony Morrice, Picton, NSW

21st July, 2003

Dear Margaret & David & Toby,

This is just a short letter. Thus far, we have enjoyed a fairly mild winter, but I'm down with either the flu' or just a cold, I'm not sure which, as my electronic thermometer was inoperative; it had been so long since I last used it (a few years) that the tiny button cell (battery) had run down. I'm not too enthusiastic about things like this that rely upon electrical power to function properly. I'll try & get an earlier model (non-battery) from a pharmacy somewhere (still used in hospitals I believe).

Knowing that you are a fairly keen gardener Margaret I thought you might enjoy the enclosed book (I also have a copy) which is full of useful tips in the garden — admittedly more focused on the kitchen garden (fruits & vegetables) I guess. Each week I watch Peter Cundall & colleagues on the Friday evening ½-hour TV programme 'Gardening Australia', & I've stored useful subjects on the VCR. I have, thus far, filled 3 × 4 HOUR video cassettes, just started volume 4. And on Sundays at 12 NOON we have on TV the one hour programme 'Landline' — more orientated towards the agricultural industry, but also some useful tips occasionally, helpful to a local gardener.

Even though there's quite hard physical work involved in garden maintenance (maybe far less if one takes onboard many of 'Pete's Mailbag' ideas & tips) I really miss not being able to have a garden — should keep one really fit too — & I don't have a workshop (which I could seriously do with), so I think I've somewhat outgrown this apartment &, as I think I previously mentioned, I'm considering selling up in the Sydney suburbs, & maybe buying a semi-rural property somewhere — probably in Australia, though I do miss the vast pine forests of Canada (though Canada has a shorter growing season) — not much opportunity to grow tropical fruits — citrus, bananas, mangoes, etc. there.

Maybe it is all but a pipe-dream; we'll see ...
Well the 4 HR video I was compiling is nearing completion — around ½ HR to go I think, & then I'll send you a copy, & also one to Ian & Margaret in Harlow; & one to a cousin of mine in Tolworth, Surbiton (this one not about gardening; it's just about the local scene).

Well, I must away for now folks. I hope you are all keeping very well there in bonny Scotland.
Bye for now.
love, Brian.

Flask foilers

Use the foil bladders of wine casks for a bird deterrent. Blow the empty foil bags up and string on the trees. If you don't drink wine ask a restaurant or such to save you a few!
Vivenne Senn, Southport, Tas

Hang it all

Use the leg of an old pantyhose or nylon stocking to store citrus fruit that is not wanted immediately. Drop one fruit down into the toe of the stocking and tie a knot; then drop the next one down and tie another knot; and so on. This keeps each fruit from touching the next. Should one go mouldy, it can be removed by slitting the mesh fabric and the rest of the crop are unaffected. Stocking toes can also be used for drying off seeds. Hang them in a warm, dry spot and as the pods pop the seed can be worked down to the bottom, where they can be removed by clipping off the toe tip and discarding the empty pods.
Jean Hooper, Maida Vale, WA

Mini Nissen Huts

I call them the mini Nissen Huts! We have found that a tin can cut in half and placed on the ground over snail pellets stops the birds eating the pellets. The pellets get to do their job and, as they keep dry, they last longer in the wet.
Stephen Taylor
Coledale, NSW

Double duty

We like to have the birds rummage amongst the mulch to collect insects but found it a nuisance as they scratched the mulch onto the paths in large quantities. By running gutter guard as shown, the mulch remains on the garden. As an added bonus leaves get trapped in the gap between the gutter guard and the path where they can be easily collected.

Wilf Clarke, Carnegie, Vic

Bagging fruit

On a small fruit tree use an old orange bag to stop birds eating the fruit. Just slip it over the whole branch of the young fruit tree and secure it with a bag tie or string. The birds hate it and won't touch the fruit.

*Alex Ray
Narooma,
NSW*

Group cover

When planting groups of seedlings cover the group with an upturned wire hanging basket, after removing the hangers. This keeps the birds and cats from scratching seedlings up. The basket can even be left over the plants if the problem persists and still look presentable.

Jan Morris, Reservoir, Vic

Quick scare

A quick, though not permanent, bird scarer can be made from old foil dishes. Tiny tart circles are just pierced and tied to a stake or small stick. Larger ones can be split and for family-pie size the following works well. Cut the dish partly into eighths. Then pierce two opposite points together and thread with a reused twist tie or twine and attach.
Marie Arelette
Yarrambat, Vic

Hologram magic

This 'Magic Eye' fixes pecking birds and allows the fruit to ripen. Cut hologram paper into strips about 7.5cm wide. Tie to tree with old nylon stocking strips. The 'eyes' flash in the sunshine and this scares the birds.
Joan Pillar
Hope Valley, SA

Wire barrier

Use wire coathangers as edging for a small garden bed. This stops dogs from scratching up the beds when you have planted new seedlings and discourages people from treading on the plants. The wire hangers also look quite attractive around the beds.
Leo & Babs Fuller-Quinn
Bondi, NSW

Net anchors

Cut suitable lengths of bird netting, thread the edges with reasonably heavy rope. When planting seedlings put stakes covered with milk cartons to stop snags, and throw the nets over. Stops white butterfly and sparrows. Is easy to throw back but the wind doesn't move it about.

Joan Murphy, Smithton, Tas

Rabbit thwarter

To stop rabbits, cut the top off a two-litre milk container. Snip the bottom so that tri-angles sit on the ground. Place stones on top to hold the container upright.

Patricia Laird
Newtown, NSW

Portable shelter

Use steel rods to construct a frame and cover it with chicken wire netting. It can be moved from place to place depending on where the young plants are coming up. It saves them being nipped off by blackbirds.

G M Fletcher, Canowindra, NSW

Bad news for birds

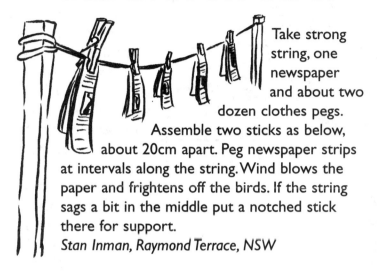

Take strong string, one newspaper and about two dozen clothes pegs. Assemble two sticks as below, about 20cm apart. Peg newspaper strips at intervals along the string. Wind blows the paper and frightens off the birds. If the string sags a bit in the middle put a notched stick there for support.

Stan Inman, Raymond Terrace, NSW

Rose ties

When you have many roses to prune, take a wheelbarrow and place a hay bale strand across it. As you cut each rose, drop it on the barrow. When the pile grows, gather the two ends and tie tightly. They are easy to handle and to stack aside.

Ruby Doherty
Penshurst, NSW

Crow catcher

To scare crows from your corn bed, take a fishing line, two stakes and several plastic bags. On either side of the corn bed put a stake. Tie the fishing line between the stakes. Cut the bottom out of the bags and cut the handles. Tie the handles of the plastic bag to the fishing line. The bag crinkles and crackles as it rustles in the wind keeping the birds away.

Cassie Rose
Lennox Head
NSW

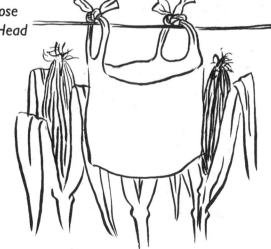

Fibre foil

To deal with birds pulling the fibre out of hanging baskets, put a pair of old pantyhose over the wire frame, tie the legs together and remove the surplus material.

Doug Bridge
Yeronga, Qld

Bag them

To grow pest-free tomatoes, when they are the size of a golf ball draw a paper bag over the bunch and twist the mouth of the bag around the stem holding the tomatoes. The tomatoes are then protected from all garden pests. They also seem to ripen quicker.

Eric Growlund
Baulkham Hills, NSW

Video hummer

My husband was recently disposing of a bad video tape, in rustling the loose tape he noticed the loud sound and distinctive reflections it gave off. He decided to try it as a bird deterrent. He strung tape about two feet above the ground, crisscrossed and twisted it to give reflections even on dull days. It gives out a vibrant 'hum' in the breeze. Now the birds have gone. We will try it out on the fruit trees next and are mildly confident it will be a goer.

Phyllis Thomson
Wyangala Dam, NSW

Bagged mulch

Spread hemp sacks over a newly mulched bed and the worms below turn the mulch over with little chance of being eaten by birds.

Boyd Zimmerman, Keilor East, Vic

Scat!

To keep cats away from your newly dug soil or freshly planted seed, soak two or three pieces of material or plastic packing in ammonia. Leave them on top of the soil.

Helen Gammage, Chapman, ACT

The eyes have it

To stop black-birds flicking the mulch out of garden beds, draw a pair of cats eyes on a scrap of wood or ice cream container. Cut to about 7-10cm square. A small nail or bit of wire coathanger will hold the stake in the ground.
John Leatham, Pascoe Vale, Vic

Clay salve

Here's a use for the clods of clay that seem to turn up unexpectedly in the garden. Keep a large margarine container with pieces of clay ready to moisten well. Whenever pruning large shrubs use a putty knife to spread the wet clay over the 'wounds'.
H Wallis, Winston Hills, NSW

Easy spreader

Use an ice-cream container with small holes punched in the bottom to spread fertiliser. It spreads evenly and you can punch holes in all or half of the bottom.
Stan Richards, Healesville, Vic

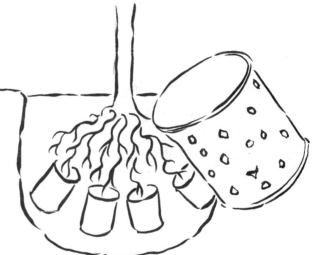

Canned citrus

A tried and tested hint for planting citrus trees in heavy clay soils. Punch holes in some steel cans (not aluminium) with the lids removed. Dig a large hole as usual for the tree, place the cans in the hole, place the tree and cover with soil as usual. The cans allow the roots to grow freely through then and when they have rusted they supply iron to the soil, thus making the fruit sweeter as well.
Marlene Gibson
Golden Grove, SA

Sock it to them

When making up liquid fertiliser out of manure, use an old sock or a pair of pantyhose (divided into two legs). Fill the leg or sock with manure and hang over the inside of a bucket of water. Attach with a clothes bag. Leave for one week and you have your own liquid fertiliser to use when you want to.

Andrew Gridley
Paralowie, SA

Blind labels

Old plastic venetian blinds make excellent labels for plants.
Sheila Redmayne, Mullaway, NSW

Spreading it

To apply fertiliser easily, use a square-shouldered plastic bucket. Cut 2cm square holes at the four compass points. Walk up and down the lawn rotating the bucket from side to side. Do wear wellingtons! If too much material is coming from the holes temporarily block up with sticky tape. Only fill half full before using. Cost—zero!

D Todd
Woodberry, NSW

Slow release

I wanted to give some new trees and shrubs a constant supply of slow-releasing fertiliser to the root system. Take a 50mm PVC pipe and insert on an angle into the same home as the plant to be planted. The pipe sits on 50mm of compost in the base of the hole and the fertiliser drops down to the roots.

Ian Leonard, Bargo, NSW

Tailor made labels

Make plant labels from 1kg yoghurt or ice cream cartons. One end can be cut to a point, but the straight-edged labels go into the ground easily enough. They can be tailor-made for size and last for a long time before deteriorating. The bottoms of the cartons can be used for plant saucers.
Elsie Elvish
Bentleigh East, Vic

Takeaway solution

Make plant labels by cutting up polyurethane trays (used in takeaways). They are easy to write on and to stick into the side of the pot.
J Lester
Sanctuary Point, NSW

Milk it

Cut up a 2-litre milk carton for plant labels. Use a soldering iron to inscribe the names on. It doesn't fade over time! Punch a hole, tie it on and it's weatherproof!
Pete Williams
Metung, Vic

Foiled

Keep the foil seal of coffee or hot chocolate tins and cut into strips to make gardening tags. Write on them with a sharp stick on a newspaper surface. A hole in the corner and a great garden tag.
Ruth McGowan, Tongala, Vic

Label saver

Use resealable food bags labelled under sections of the garden to store plant tags. They're easy to update.
Marion Payne
Pymble West, NSW

Days of our lives

When we moved into our house the previous owner gave me her garden diary. This book contained a plan of all her garden beds (numbered) and through this book were the days she planted, where she pruned, etc. I have continued with the idea and this book has been a great help to me. I am able to go back through and see when to transplant strawberry runners, prune the boysenberries, etc.

Barbara Wheeler, Tarcutta, NSW

Clipped

Use all those bread bag clips as labels. They are easy to write on with a marker pen and clip firmly to the side of almost any pot—great for seed trays and propagating trays.

Ann Breeding
Burra, NSW

Avoiding the blades

Flowers, like daffodils, look very natural when growing in clumps on a lawn. It can be difficult keeping them free of weeds and cut the grass around them. You could grow them in pots as follows. Dig a hole in the lawn. Place pot in it with a drainage layer of pebbles under it. A mower should be able to cut across the top of this pot. Take a separate pot, of the same size, containing the flowers and place in the ground pot. Stand it on a block to avoid jamming. This pot can be lifted out when the lawn is being cut and afterwards replaced.

Jim Quantrill
Isabella Plains, ACT

A rolling success

Use the cardboard inner cores of toilet rolls as pots to plant seeds in. When the seedlings are big enough, plant them core and all into the garden. The core soon rots away and the plant does not suffer any setback. Using this method even root crops like parsnips can be transplanted.
Brian Clark
Chum Creek, Vic

Germinator

Germinate seeds in a poly-styrene box with the seed tray sitting on a hot water bottle. When the seeds have germinated change the lid for a clear plastic sheet.
Laurie Thompson
Mount Waverley, Vic

Saving and sowing tomato seeds

Save tomato seeds for later planting by squeezing the seeds onto an opened paper lunchbag. Spread them roughly even and close and flatten the bag. Write the seed name and date on bag and hang up in the shed until dry. Fold and file until needed. Come planting time open the bag and place in garden bed, cover lightly with soil and keep moist. You will have plenty of seedlings for yourself and friends.
Barry Selwood, Endeavour Hills, Vic

Mini greenhouse

The little clear plastic boxes alfalfa sprouts come in make miniature greenhouses for special seeds. Easy and light to use, they have small drain holes in the base of the container.
Joan Turner
Mandurah, WA

Bulb finder

I mark the position of bulb clumps by planting several grape hyacinths around each group of daffodils, jonquils, snow-drops, etc. These hardy little bulbs are first out of the ground in January, soon after the old bulb leaves have disappeared. When I see them I know not to dig near that spot. I have used this system of natural markers for 30 years and it's a great success. As well as being a useful marker the pretty blue flowers are a nice contrast to the other coloured bulbs.
Nancy Wells
O'Connor, ACT

Bulb base

Collect your egg cartons and store bulbs away inside them. Easy to store and envi-ronmentally friendly.
Leeta Spinola
Old Guildford, NSW

Instant greenhouse

For a miniature green-house for tomatoes, cut a plastic shopping bag across the bottom and place it around a chrysan-themum holder. Tie bag handles to the top of the stand.
Julie Davidson
Lower Mitcham, SA

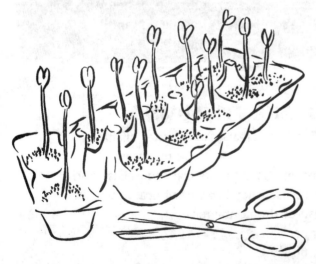

Egg planters

Egg cartons are useful seedboxes. When seedlings are a reasonable size, the carton can be cut and seedlings easily removed. Otherwise they can be soaked overnight, cut and transplanted with the cardboard (soaked). The cardboard soon disintegrates.
K Thomas
Wentworth Falls, NSW

Tomato bagger

Take a standard plastic shopping bag by the handles. Swing the bag over the tomato stake 'ballooning' the bag and impaling it down over the stake. Continue to slide the bag down to ground level to create a tent over the tomato seedling. You can use a small amount of dirt to secure the edges around the seedling. Next day, pull the bag up carefully off the seedling and slide to the top of the stake. Secure with a rubber band until the next cold night. It also makes a great racket in the wind and scares birds away.
Jos van der Velde, Downer, ACT

Anchored seedlings

Keep seedlings in place until they root and stop blackbirds eating them by placing a rock or half brick next to them. The birds cannot scratch and it also helps seedlings form strong roots as moisture is retained and the sun kept off the ground. Almost anything heavy enough to discourage birds works—cement, large clods of earth, etc.
Verity Stewart
Mooroopna, Vic

In the can

The little plastic containers that photographic films come in are great for storing seeds.
Sue Curtis, Yambuna, Vic

Hiding the Hills

After our kids had swung on the Hills Hoist for about 20 years it developed a few unwanted curves. We bought a new hoist and turned the old one into a shadehouse with some barlon cloth, tubing and batons. We cut down an old fly-screen door for the entrance and put some shelves around the sides.
Ray Warland, Bilgola Plateau, NSW

Sunshade

Cut part of the side out of a plant pot. Place over young plant. This allows it to get the morning sun but cuts out the midday sun.

Wendy Furminger
Acacia Ridge, Qld

Bag it

Take a clear plastic clothes storage bag. Place several seedling trays inside, water and zip up. Watch the plants grow. They will hold enough seed trays to plant an average vegetable garden. They also make good frost covers for potplants.

Jan Manz, Loxton, SA

Lime bait

Instead of using snail bait, which is harmful to dogs, sprinkle bricklayers' lime around the edges of your plot. Or mix a third of a cup of the lime to one litre of water, shake up and spray on the shrubs. In 24 hours, no snails.

Ted Rennie, Rosebud, Vic

Cutting care

Carry cuttings in plastic takeaway containers filled with green florists' foam, which has been thoroughly soaked in water. Cuttings are still fresh at the end of the day.

Jeanette Lee
Adamstown Heights, NSW

Seed separator

Separate seeds from the plant material using an old seive. Some vigorous shaking, a couple of good taps and all the precious seeds fall through on to your piece of paper.

Jacqueline Lightbody, Mitcham, SA

Stakeout

To avoid splinters on garden stakes, smooth the four edges by electric grinder, sander or a carpenter's plane. Protect the top of the stake using a preserved-fruit tin with its top and bottom removed. Then cut the can down the middle and flatten it out. Cut strips width-wise approximately 3cm wide, wrap a strip around the top of the stake and secure with a small nail. Preserve stakes by painting them with a solution of one litre of waste sump oil mixed with approximately half a cup of kerosene. The stakes last for many years with this treatment.
Allon Hofmoun
Toowoomba, Qld

Milk magic

Here's how to use three sections of a plastic milk bottle.
Geoff Howe
Rosedale, NSW

Instant shadehouse

Make a shade-house using four star pickets and half a sheet of reomesh. Cover with plastic or shadecloth.

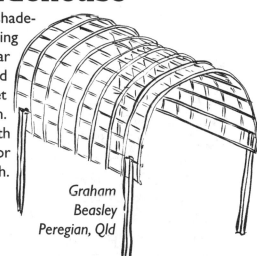

Graham Beasley
Peregian, Qld

Don't rubbish the bin

Use an old large plastic bin for compost. Cut the bottom out, turn upside down and use a small-size lid on the new 'top'. Tie wire on the handles and over the top of the lid to stop it blowing off. To turn compost lift the bin off, turn compost over and place the bin back on the pile. There is no problem with flies.
Audrey Wombold
Ballina, NSW

Pill box

Use plastic or glass pill bottles to store seeds from one season to the next.
Eric Quinn
Taree, NSW

Quick guard

Make gaiters out of your old gum-boots. These protect the lower legs from injury and keep grass off your socks.
John Lowe
Steels Creek, Vic

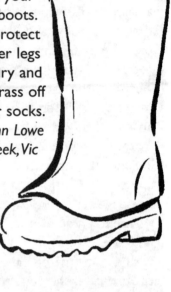

Bean there

When planting French beans dig a trench about a spade's depth. Fork fertiliser into it. Put a layer of soil above this and plant the bean seeds in this layer. As the plants grow, fill in the trench around them up to the lowest pair of leaves. When they are fully grown they are still in a very shallow trench only a couple of centimetres deep. They can be watered by irrigation, saving overhead watering and a lot of water!
William MIller
Hawthorn, SA

Thornguard

Cut the tops and bottoms off two milk cartons. Then when you are pruning roses or prickly bushes slide the milk cartons over your forearms and then pull on your gloves. No scratches from thorns, or hooked seeds in your jumper.
Geoff Walker
Lismore
NSW

Bird scarer

It's easy to make a bird scarer out of a plastic bottle. Cut it to make fins as shown.
E Edwards
Wynnum, QLD

Seed shelter

Plant seeds then place pieces of 3cm stakes along the row. Put a plank on top until seedlings show.
Edith Morrison
Glen Innes, NSW

Drip share

The new dripping hoses made from recycled car tyres are terrific and a great way to give good deep watering but they are expensive. To cut costs I place them only where I need them to wet the roots and join the inbetween bits with ordinary black poly pipe that is used for drip systems, etc. Most people have got some of this hose left over.
Tom Laber, Eltham, Vic

Light the way

Here's a simple low cost way to light your garden at night. Cut off the bottom of a clear plastic bottle. Shave a candle's base till it fits into the bottle neck. Push into the ground. If you want the light on a flat surface, nail the bottle cap to a suitably sized piece of wood and screw onto the bottle.
Raymond Taylor
Darwin, NT

Catchment system

Catching rainwater from the garage roof into a holding tank can help spread the valuable moisture through the garden with a simple piping system.
Cyril Heming-Lynch
Corrimal, NSW

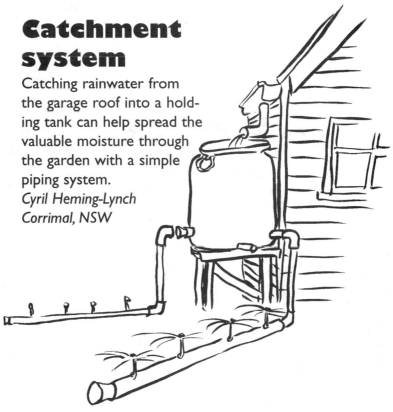

Salt circles nail snails

Run a circle of salt around plants that are
being attacked by snails. By the next day
the snails will be dead as they can't get
any traction and salt burns them.
Lorraine Brown
Old Beach, Tas

Pipe streams

This idea saves moving the hose so
often when you don't want to disturb
new seedlings. Take a length of plastic pipe, about
90mm diameter, big enough to take the hose. Drill holes along the length of
the pipe and make legs from pipe halves as shown.
Les Trice, Noraville, NSW

Glass cover

Take a two-litre glass flag-
gon bottle. Freeze in
freezer. Take out, set in
sink and carefully
pour boiling
water in. The
bottom seal
gives way and
you have a glass
cloche.
Marc Valentine
Redfern, NSW

Goodnight possum

We had a very determined possum in the roof space who always
managed to find a spot out of our
reach to bunk down. I concluded
since it went out every night, I
would try changing night to day.
So I installed a low cost fluores-
cent light in the roof areas. The
possum disappeared. That was
1995 and no new invaders have
arrived.
Albert Waite
Old Bar, NSW

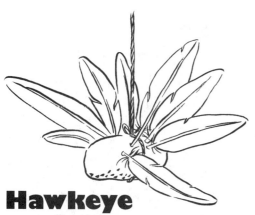

Hawkeye

Scare birds off your fruit trees by making your own hawk. Take a potato and stick some feathers in it. Tie the potato securely with string and hang on the tree where the wind will turn it around.
D Ewence
Mentone, Vic

Deepwater tactics

To grow garden vegetables, sink a 25-30cm plastic pot in prepared area, manured deeply. Plant seeds around the circumference of the pot. Put a couple of handfuls of grass or straw loosely in the pot. Always water inside the pot. The roots go deep and get water at root level as required.
J Godwin
Ballarat, Vic

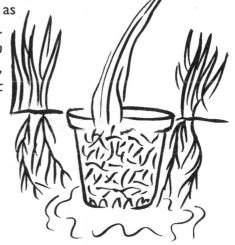

Clog comfort

For those gardeners who dislike wearing gum boots try clogs. Paint a plain pair a few times with linseed oil and turpentine to water-proof them. They are warm in winter, easy to slip on and off and cheap.
Grace Holroyd
Rivett, ACT

Gutterguard cage

I have constructed a plant cage out of gut-terguard and four pieces of dowelling, two widths for the height and two widths for the top, all tied together with twine.
Tess Kloot, Box Hill North, Vic

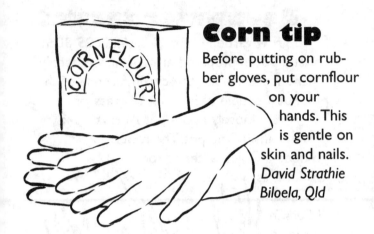

Corn tip

Before putting on rubber gloves, put cornflour on your hands. This is gentle on skin and nails.
David Strathie
Biloela, Qld

Self destruction

Bindweed, with its long roots, is very difficult to kill. Try the following. Collect together as many tendrils of the plant as you can. Bundle these up and stuff them into a plastic bag. Tie up the bag and leave for a week or two so the poison is absorbed back down the weed's system. The weed will be dead within a week and no damage is done to the surrounding plantlife or pets.
Roger Kirkby
Emu Park, Qld

Easy kneeler

I collect all plastic wrappings that the newspapers are delivered in. Roll them tightly into balls. Take two 3kg orange net plastic bags. Place them one inside the other for strength and stuff them very tightly with the plastic balls. Tie the bag with string and make a large loop handle so the kneeler can be stored or carried about.
Eva Booth
Wollongong, NSW

Corker of an idea

Collect wine corks. Put them in a stocking or net orange bag. Place them like sausages under wooden borders to act as drainage stones and help keep wood dry at base.
Eva Booth
Wollongong, NSW

Sugar boost

I have successfully transferred 15 tree ferns over 20 years. Every six months I place a handful of sugar in the middle of the tree and water it. The energy in the sugar makes the ferns grow extra well.
Diane Koszek
Chipping Norton, NSW

Finding fresh ground

My problem was tomatoes that needed to be moved to a different spot every year. There weren't many sunny spots left in the garden that I hadn't used, so I decided to give them new soil. Buy a good bag of potting mix, add a bit of chicken poo. Mix in well. Split the bag lengthwise and find a suitable spot to put it. A few drainage holes in the base and plant your seedlings in the top split.

Jane Hall, Trigg, WA

Barrow clip

I always have difficulty getting the contents of my wheelbarrow into a plastic garbage bag. Recently I was so frustrated when the bag kept collapsing on me that I grabbed a couple of clothes pegs and pegged the bag to the wheelbarrow. This left my two hands free to scrape the contents into the garbage bag.
Helen Clift
O'Halloran Hill, SA

Leaf broom

Use an old broom handle and cut it to the length of a walking stick. Put three or four nails in that end and cut off nail heads. You have a handy tool for picking up leaves.
Bernard & Joyce Wood
Batchelor, NT

Low carrier

Use an old skateboard for a trolley when moving large plant pots around your home or garden. It is strong, low to the ground for easy loading and easy to manoeuvre round corners indoors or outside.
Gordon Winter, Greenwood, WA

Dags to the rescue

A useful tip for anyone who has access to fleece—save all the 'dag' ends and really dirty parts of the fleece and use these as mulch. They make a wonderful anti-weed carpet and also supply a bonus of nutrients from the manure left on the wool. Slugs find it difficult to move around on the wool. Also, the leaves of lettuce, etc, are kept clean and free of soil. Furthermore fleece can be used as mulch on potplants and hanging baskets—the plants are extra snug during the colder months, with their pure wool insulation!
Margaret Pawson
Tivoli, Qld

Safe stakes

To make stakes safe to use in the garden. Cut the bottoms off plastic drink bottles but keep the lids on. Pop a bottle on the top of each stake.
V C Smith
Rainbow, Vic

Steamroller

Kill weeds along the fenceline or in paving by pouring a kettle of boiling water straight over them.
F G Brumpton
McKinnon, Vic

Mow & mulch

As the leaves fall, they are mowed to save raking them up. They are then ready for the compost heap or as mulch around the shrubs.
Lynne Robson
Esk, Qld

Star bolter

Remove star pickets or reo steel pegs using a pair of boltcutters.
Clive Wood
Narangba, Qld

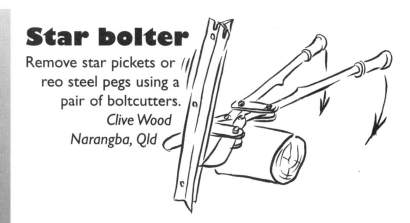

Blade weeder

When you break a hacksaw blade turn it into a versatile weeding tool. Put a handle of hose or tape on it. It

cuts through stalks or tap roots of broad leaf weeds; is a weeder that grips the very fine roots of couch, etc., and allows easier removal; is excellent for weeding around small delicate plants and doesn't blunt.
Kevin McMullen, Vacy, NSW

Roll up

Here's an easy way to gather garden debris and then get it into a rubbish bag.
Richard Forster
Eden, NSW

Compost the annuals

When summer or winter annuals are finished place them loosely on the lawn and run the rotary lawn mower over them. Mix the chopped up mixture with lawn clippings and some dampened horse manure. Woody plants and prunings can also be added. Turn the heap every three to four days and the compost is ready in a fortnight.
Allon Hofmoun
Toowoomba, Qld

Framed

To protect the microclimate spray system, surround the uprights with frames made from plastic bottles cut as shown.
Paul Mainwaring
Willetton, WA

Add-on power

To make weed pulling less painful, extend your hand weeder by tying it firmly to a broom handle and bending it to a 120° angle.
Anthony Vucak
Swan View, WA

Rapid compost

Kitchen waste rapidly decomposes in ordinary plastic supermarket bags. Then dig the lovely black sticky stuff directly into the soil.
Jean Burton, Wentworth Falls, NSW

Low cart

Use an old motor-mower frame as a low-to-the-ground cart for heavy pots, bricks, etc.
Lillian Godfrey
Mareeba, Qld

Hot revival

When your plastic rake has almost worn straight. Apply gentle heat from the porta-gas and use a pair of long nose pliers to make a 'new' rake.
Bruce Sinclair
Wentworthville, NSW

Baby power

A use for the now defunct baby walkers. Put a bucket in the centre to cart manure etc round the garden.
Beryl Turner
Frankston, Vic

Sharp act

I had my garden spade altered by a local engineering company. The corners were cut off and raw edges smoothed. It is now pointed and can penetrate soil, sawdust etc much easier than before. It is also lighter and easier to use.
Kath Wray
Armidale
NSW

Balloon trickler

Put a small hole in the top of a balloon. Attach over the spout of a watering can. You can trickle weedkiller between paving slabs where weeds are growing.
Daphne Stephenson
Ferndale, Vic

Shopping ties

Cut the handles off a shopping bag and you have two long ties for staking flowers and trees, etc.
Eona McCourt
Wyoming, NSW

Insect kick

A few squirts of an aerosol flyspray into the airtake of a troublesome mower will 'kick-start' it.
Douglas, Mary & Lorraine Brown
Old Beach, Tas

New for old

Don't throw away that broken spade handle. If it is 30-40cm long it is ideal for ramming the soil around a newly planted plant. Also it is great for leaning on, to help you stand in a tight corner where there is nothing else to hang on to.
Joan Smith
Chelsea, Vic

Swollen tight

If the heads on your garden tools are loose, submerge them in water overnight. They swell up in the water and stay tight for a long time.
Joan &
Allan
Hunter
Pakenham
Vic

Salvaging strawberry runners

To take strawberry runners from the main plant, take one plastic cup or margarine container. Make a half-inch slit down one side of the cup and another opposite it. Fill the cup with potting mix and make a dimple in the middle. Place strawberry runner in. Open one slit slightly and put runner stalk through. In the opposite slit put a leaf through it. This anchors the plant down. In a couple of weeks roots form and you can snip the new plant from the mother plant.
Sandra McKean
Mount Seymour, Tas

Soft blast

When repairing the black plastic pipes of your watering system, use a hairdryer to help attach them to various sprays. Blast the dryer on the pipes for a few seconds and they become more malleable.
Peter Bateman
Burnside, SA

A right scrubber

Hammer a new scrubbing brush into a piece of wood—bristles facing up! Butt the board against a wall. Put one foot on the board to hold it and clean the other foot on the bristles. Much cheaper than buying a boot cleaner.
Kim Terhorst
Strathfield North, NSW

Dropper stoppers

I use short pieces of steel droppers hammered into the ground to stop the hose from dragging across garden beds. For safety we slice a slit in an old tennis ball and place it on the steel droppers.
Norma Clapp, Peterborough, SA

Orchid nursery

To grow Australian native orchids, cut a two-litre plastic milk carton in half. Put a handful of sphagnum moss in the bottom. Place the top half of bottle on top with cap removed. Top up with water occasionally. Place the top piece of orchid neck down inside it. Plant in a pot when the roots form strongly enough.
A Patterson
North Rocks, NSW

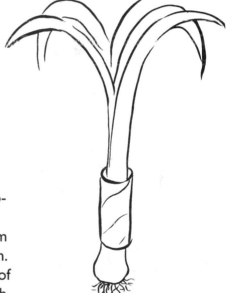

Rolled for blanching

Grow leeks in the cardboard part of a toilet roll. Add another above as it gets taller. This keeps the stalks nice and white.
C Goldie
Kilsyth, Vic

Of cabbages and slugs

For slug and cut worm control. Lay several large leaves off brassica plants on your vegie garden. In the morning pick up and shake into a bucket.
Chris Polgasse
Tanja, NSW

Soft touch

Use old hot water bottles as kneeling pads for the house and garden. Empty water out and stuff with old stockings or soft material.
Eva Haebich
Elsternwick, Vic

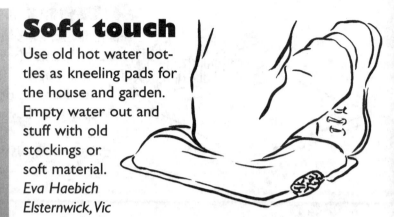

Low rider

A sawn-off front fork and handlebars, block of hardwood and two foam pads glued on make a commercial garden kneeler. It is fully adjustable for height and angle and the handlebars actually support the thighs when kneeling.
Richard Ward
Kensington Park, SA

Boxed in

These garden boxes are made from treated pine and lined with plastic. keep two inches of water in the trough so you don't have to water every day. You can mow underneath them, there's easy weeding at eye level, and they're snail and slug proof.
J M Byrnes
Evans Head, NSW

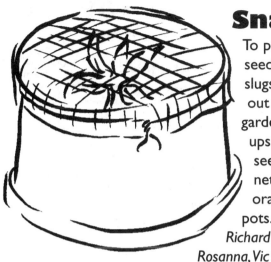

Snail cover

To protect vulnerable seedlings from snail and slugs, cut the bottom out of an old plastic garden pot and place it upside down over the seedlings. Put some netting (e.g. from orange bags) over the pots.

Richard Burgess
Rosanna, Vic

Quick measures

The difficulty of measuring small amounts of insecticide spray for just one or two plants, can be easily overcome by using a small hypodermic syringe (without the needle) to draw up the liquid directly from the bottle. Especially good is a reusable glass syringe from your doctor, or a well-stocked hobby shop, where they use them to measure the fuel for model aircraft engines.

J Jones, Lake Cathie, NSW

Fly in, stay put

Here's an easy-to-make fruit-fly catcher made out of two bottles.

C A Leer
Ryde, NSW

Lateral thinking for green manure

I've always wanted to grow green manure but was put off by having to dig it in. Instead I sow the seeds in shallow poly-boxes, add wood-ash from the fire and any old soil that needs enriching. Turn the box upside down on the bed when the time comes.

I Manz
Bellingen, NSW

Fruit fly trap

Use a small glass jar with a hole about 10cm diameter in the lid and some light wire. The bait is two teaspoons of vinegar and a teaspoon of honey mixed and dissolved in a half cup of warm water. The trap is suspended on a wire tied around the upper end of the jar. This allows it to hang at a 45-degree angle. A few of these traps may be placed at strategic spots around the garden and fruit fly will come from miles around to get them.

Arthur Hill, Marks Point, NSW

Homely mozzie zapper

To deter mosquitoes from breeding in the plants, put diluted pine disinfectant in a squeeze bottle. Give each plant a squirt!
*R Bown
Tuchekoi, Qld*

Toad oil

Place two or three drops of tea-tree oil on a cane toad's back and it will be dead within a short time.
*Darryl Watson
Sunnybank Hill
Qld*

Trapped

Another simple insect and wasp catcher.
*Nan Smead
Balwyn, Vic*

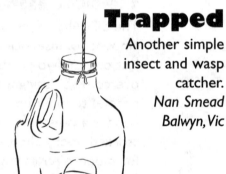

Petproof snail catcher

For gardeners who hate snails but have pets, take a used beer can (with a little in the bottom). Enlarge the hole making it large enough for a snail to get in. Drop a few snail pellets in. Put the can in the garden under a shrub or bush. In a few days it will be full of dead snails.
Jean Goadby, Manning, WA

Travelling easy

Use an old luggage rack as a spray carrier so it can be wheeled around instead of carried.
S Evans,
Boorowa, NSW

Hose holder

Keep two-litre plastic bottles with a handle, filled with water, at different spots around the garden. When a special plant needs watering they can be used for holding the hose in the right direction.
Mrs M Finlay, Ourimbah, NSW

Charcoal power

When propagating I found fine sand and crushed charcoal obtained a better result than any other type of mixture. Also, crushed charcoal enhanced the growth of plants when added to potting mixtures. Dipping plant cuttings in charcoal powder is as good as using striking powder.
A E Blundell
Moss Vale, NSW

Easy seat

Make a garden seat using a sleeper and a set of old concrete tub legs. Finish off with a coat of outdoor paint.
Pam & Ray Rohneshing, Morayfield, Qld

Slug & snail solution

Make a super snail and slug trap with a used orange juice bottle and some snail bait. Lie the bottle on the ground. Put a stake through the centre of the bottle to hold it in the ground. Place some snail bait inside.
Trevor Jessop
Upper Beaconsfield, Vic

Mini greenhouses

Save all plastic cordial bottles. Cut the bottoms out with scissors, and place them, after removing the screw cap, over the seedlings. Place the label side away from the sun to reflect the low-angled sunlight onto the back of the plant. The temperature builds up nicely and creates a mini-hothouse effect. (A stake can go down through the bottle to anchor it.)

Noelene & Barry Allen
Oyster Cove, Tas

Hear, hear

Pack several empty 425g tins with dried grass or straw. These are inverted on short sticks and placed in the garden. Every day or so the straw is taken out and the earwigs can be tapped out of the tin. The tins and straw can then be reused.

Harry Shrubshall
Coburg, Vic

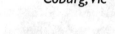

Easy drips

Recycle plastic two-litre bottles. Punch a hole in the end. Fill with water. Stand behind plants, making a drip system for plants that dry out quickly in heat and wind.

Dianne Galloway
Belrose, NSW

Spot weeding

Keep empty paste bottles with the brush in the lid. Pour herbicides into the bottles. When you want to 'spot' weeds the brush is right where you need it to paint the poison on.
*Miriam Tonkin
Somerton Park, SA*

Gimme shelter

Cut the bottom out of five-litre paint tins. Place round tomato plants to give them shelter.
*Jim & Nancy Horrocks
Port Noarlunga, SA*

Bag 'em

Use 'grow bags' to grow tomatoes in. You can easily make your own. Bags of potting mix are specially formulated with essential nutrients and fertilisers. You could try quality potting mix, compost, cow manure and slow-release fertiliser. Puncture the bags in the bottom for drainage.
Michael Lawless, Seacombe, Vic

Scraps bring in the worms

Save vegetable scraps each day and then every morning dig them into the soil. In a vegetable garden it is a good idea to dig them into the spaces between the rows of plants. Scraps can be added to soil and then a new row of plants put in beside it. Scraps can also be dug in around plants and trees in the rest of the garden—be careful to avoid the roots! This process encourages vast numbers of worms and takes only five minutes each day.
Catherine Lyons, Tumbulgum, NSW

Funnel ease

Cut the neck off a two-litre plastic juice bottle and use as a funnel when filling jars with home-made jam and chutneys.

Margaret Jacobs
Kendenup, WA

Hangup

I had trouble keeping the extension cord for my mower from getting tangled up. I use off-cuts of plastic mesh. This idea can also be used for hoses.

Doreen Leech
Loch Sport, Vic

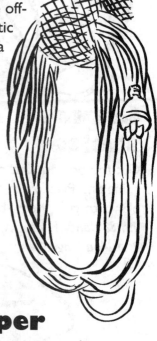

Big dripper

Take four-litre oil containers with the top cut off, washed in hot water and detergent. A small hole is bored near the bottom of each container. These can be filled with a watering can, hose or bucket. I also use 10-litre buckets with holes for larger plants.

David Woods
Kingaroy, Qld

Mulching comfort

Use 'op-shop' woollen blankets (preferably tartan for sumptuous effect) as a mulch mat for suppressing weeds and holding in the moisture. Cover with extra compost.
Anna Perry, Cottesloe, WA

Mini master

Make mini portable sprinkler systems for parts of the garden where it is difficult to insert a permanent one. Use some mini portable systems from the leftovers of a sprinkler kit. Take some pieces of 3x2 scrap timber and fit pieces of sprinkler hose to them with the end fittings to fit onto normal snap-on hose fittings. You can make any size or combination to suit your needs.

Michael Davis, Penrith, NSW

Lighten up

Get light into the dark corners of your garden by using glass or tin foil to reflect into them.
John Hamilton
St Kilda, SA

Instant watering can

Get an empty jam or fruit tin and punch holes in the bottom with a hammer and nail. You have a mini watering can.
Vi Blunden
Petrie, Qld

Getting high

Take a plastic milk bottle and drill small holes in the lid. Fill bottle with fertiliser or water and use like a squeeze bottle to water difficult to reach hanging baskets.
Martin Pinchback
Albany, WA

Wick bladder

Fill a wine cask bladder with water or liquid fertiliser. Push a piece of cotton rag or wick into the opening and bury near your plant. This will give you a drip feeder system for up to two weeks.
Ginger Gibson
Nimbin, NSW

Quick protection

Here's a quick solution for protecting young plants.
Brian Peach
Tiaro, Qld

Pumped up

To clean micro-jets. Screw them into a bicycle pump and pump the dirt out. If this doesn't rid the obstruction push a piece of fine wire through and pump again.
R Manuel
Turners Beach, Tas

Pantyhose revival

Stuff old pantyhose with newspaper, rags, old clothing or anything that will absorb water. Soak them in a bucket of water. Make up a liquid fertiliser and soak them in it overnight. They have many uses, e.g. lay them around your plants, dig a trench around scrubs and bury to retain moisture, hang them over your pot-plants so water drips on them.
Ken Carpenter
Payneham, SA

Scale brush

When cleaning scale and fungus off roses use a long-handled bottle brush which has stiff plastic bristles.
Joy Jones
Mona Vale, Tas

Stocking trap

Put snail and slug pellets in a stocking and wrap it around a tree's trunk. This forms a physical barrier the snails do not want to cross. Also, the rain leeches out pellets over the trunk below the stocking, further discouraging the snails.
Murray Howlett
Granville, NSW

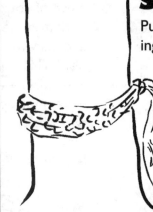

Facesaver

When spraying high fruit trees fix spray handle to a broom handle. This saves spray in the face.
Derek & Jean Kent
Mordialloc, Vic

Sandy soil solution

The following is very useful for slowing down the quick drying-out of soil in sandy areas. Take a 1m length of 5cm PVC piping. Bore holes with a brace about 10cm apart so water can come out all around. Make your first hole about 15cm above the ground end. Insert your pipe into the ground alongside your shrub or tree leaving 10cm above ground. Tie your plant to the pipe with a strip of pantyhose. Pour water into the pipe until it flows out of the holes above the ground. At first water will flow out everywhere but when the ground becomes thoroughly wet the water will begin to stay and seep gently, keeping the soil around it moist for days.
Margaret Cobley
Geraldton, WA

Pot holder

Take a 20cm plastic flower pot and screw it to a post or fence. It can be used as an easy holder for hoses.
Kym Webb
Aldinga Beach, SA

Honeywell

To make a honeywell, cut a plastic bottle in halves, then cut half an inch off the top and remove lid. Turn it upside down, set plant in and water.
Kath Mawhood
Port Augusta, SA

Net news

A very efficient compost bin can be made from netting and newspaper. Use short lengths of 12-inch rabbit repair-netting and build the one-metre-high heap by easy stages. Join a circle of netting about 1x1.5 metres in diameter, and line it with sheets of folded news-paper, supported against the netting with a series of small stakes. Just keep adding weeds, herbs, kitchen scraps, manures, seaweeds, etc., until it has reached the top of the first netting ring. Remove the stakes and add another layer of netting and a further lining of newspaper, overlapping the first row. Again, it may be necessary to hold it with stakes until it fills out. When it reaches the required height poke holes around in the paper to aerate the heap and leave it to settle to about two-thirds of the finished height. Remove the netting, and shred the paper, placing it onto the ground nearby and turning the heap onto it. The compost should be ready to use in about three weeks from turning.
Jean Hooper
Maida Vale, WA

Easy lifting

Having many times put a spade through a bulb when lifting, I have finally found a cure. I plant them out over a hessian base filling the hole.
June Towers
Tumby Bay, SA

Cat foiler

To keep cats from using pots as toilets, place a hanging basket liner or shade cloth on top of the soil around the plant. This also serves as mulch for the plants in summer.
Margaret Tobin
Burton, SA

Shaky perch

Stop birds defecating on plants supported by stakes, e.g., toma-toes. Install a plat-form using a nail with a 5mm gap between the head of the nail and the top of the stake. When the bird lands on the plat-form, the platform moves and the bird flies away.
Peter Costa
St Albans, NSW

Neighbourly barrier

There is a simple remedy for any patch of garden that is doing poorly because the roots of trees or shrubs from next door have infiltrated under the fence and are taking the nourishment. By digging down and inserting an old sheet of galvanised iron lengthwise, you can extend the fence bottom and exclude the roots.
Bob Chalmers
Como, NSW

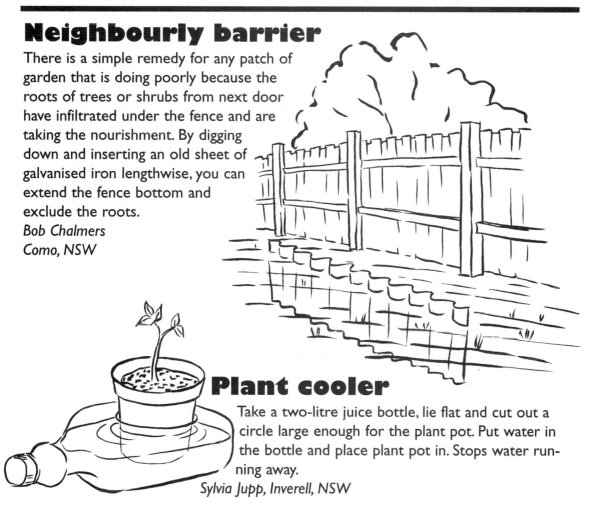

Plant cooler

Take a two-litre juice bottle, lie flat and cut out a circle large enough for the plant pot. Put water in the bottle and place plant pot in. Stops water running away.
Sylvia Jupp, Inverell, NSW

Icy drips

I fill up two-litre juice containers almost full and freeze them. When I go out on a particularly hot day, I set a frozen bottle of ice near any special little seedling and it drips away for about 36 hours.
Margo Woodcock
Halls Gap, Vic

Cheapstakes

For a cheap way to stake plants to protect them in windy weather, open out wire coathangers, straighten them and cut in half. Make a stake with an almost closed ring at the top. Push into the ground without disturbing the roots too much.
Dawn Rabone
Kaniva, Vic

Spacesaver

To save space in the garden where there is no trellis, use small tree limbs with plenty of branches.
Phil Jones
Koonawarra, NSW

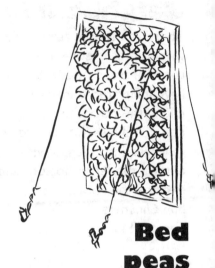

Bed peas

I grow my sweet peas on an old single bed and I get wonderful flowers, up to two metres high.
Jack Swain
Colac, Vic

Pipe coat

Cut 10mm mild steel to length required and push this through an old garden hose. It is much more attractive than plain pipe.
Neil Rahn
Berry, NSW

Weeds—a true story

I had planted carrot seeds, and had been told not to spray them to keep the weeds down until just as the third fern shoot appeared, or the carrots could be affected by the spray. So as not to miss my timing, I watched their growth carefully, and each morning and afternoon I would survey them minutely—and would pull out the odd weed as it appeared. Eventually the third fern shoot was showing. BUT by then there were no weeds in sight—and I didn't need to spray at all!
Loftus Dun
Oatley, NSW

Video bandage

Use old video cassette tape to bind split branches. It's tough, durable, long lasting, waterproof and ties perfectly.
Len Edwards
Glen Waverley, Vic

Stake planter

For an easy way to drive stakes into the ground, take a length of water pipe approximately 80cm long by 20cm in diameter. Thread one end and fit a 20cm screw cap. Stand stake in one hand and slip open end of pipe over the stake. Lift pipe as high as possible before allowing pipe to freefall.
Owen Blattman
Camden, NSW

Coming to grips with onion weed

To get rid of onion weed, get a bit of 5cm PVC pipe and saw 'teeth' around one end. Push or twist it over the weed until it's below the bulb. Trial and error will give you the depth setting. When you are deep enough give the pipe a few rotations. Extract the plug and dispose of it where it won't regrow.
Geoff Walker, Mallabula, NSW

The killer glove

To kill weeds growing near plants, mix some glyphosate. Put on a rubber glove, then put a cotton or other absorbent glove over it. Wet glove with glyphosate, making sure it doesn't drip. Grasp weed or grass low down (taking care not to touch nearby plants) and draw carefully to the top.
Geoff Hillman
Kew, NSW

Spray control

To get around the problem of drifting spray when you're tackling weeds. Cut the bottom out of a two-litre juice container and unscrew the cap. Place it over the weed then insert the sprayer into the top. Only the weed gets the treatment and the person spraying is also protected.
Ann Moore
Turramurra, NSW

Chiseller

Use a 2cm chisel to weed the lawn and garden. You can dig close to a plant without damaging it.
Marj Allerton
Tamworth, NSW

Stepping stones

Make cement stepping blocks to use in large gardens among the plants for stepping onto weed or for decorative use. Cut 8cm-wide strips of flooring vinyl and cut them to the required size. Overlap ends about 8cm and join with soft wire. They can be coloured brown with oxide. When dry undo the wire and reuse a bag of ready mix.
Joy Timmins
Upper Mount Gravatt, Qld

Post lifter

To remove a steel star post that is too tight to wiggle out, put a bolt through one of the lowest holes. Then with a small log of wood, place the log underneath a solid length of timber. Place one end of the timber underneath the bolt. If the steel post is a bit tight it might pay to drill a small hole through the timber near the steel post. Tie a piece of wire through the hole and around the steel post just below the bolt to stop it slipping. Then a see-saw, action should send the steel post out of the ground.
Jerry Morris
Carlton Beach, Tas

Knee help

A styrofoam fruit or vegetable box can make a great kneeling pad for use when the ground is damp.
Joan Faulkner
Evatt, ACT

Soil saver

Use a discarded plastic shower curtain to make dumping soil easier after digging a hole. Fold the first 30cm under and place the fold at the edge of the proposed hole. When the curtain is dragged away the tucked-under part unfolds to catch any soil that gravitates to the rear.

A S Bannerman
Rostrevor, SA

Soaped

Put soap in an onion bag and hang from the garden tap. It dries out quickly and the bag mesh gives a slight friction if you have grease or paint on your hands.

Joyce Kirkham, Chester Hill, NSW

Versatile hose

Plastic garden hose nozzles can be made into a variety of 'custom' sprinklers with very little effort. Strip off the outside nozzle which is rotated to vary the water jet use. This reveals the spigot, which has either two or four holes. Make a simple stand from a length of aluminium double-groove track for sliding insect screens with a clip fashioned from heavy gauge wire. The bottom end of the aluminium is ground to a V-shaped point for insertion into the soil. When a four-hole spigot is attached to the hose and clipped into the wire clip in a vertical position, it makes an excellent all-round water sprinkler. When a two-hole spigot is used, it sprinkles in a straight line. You can also reshape the holes on a couple of spigots to give a different watering pattern. The outside nozzle can be screwed on again for normal hand watering.

Frank Moran
Tarragindi, Qld

In-line sanity

When watering you don't need to kink the hose to temporarily stop water flow as you move about the garden. Insert an 'in-line' tap about three or four metres from the outlet end of the hose.
Rob Broadbridge, Narangba, Qld

Tea lift

Save all used teabags and feed them to your plants. They do an excellent job.
G Willers
Bensleigh, Qld

Easy hoop

Bend fencing wire into a loop, leaving 7cm to push into the ground. This holds up floppy, tall, flowering stems.
Dorothy & Jim Watt
Briagolong, Vic

Basket hanger

Make a coathanger into a basket hanger. 1. Pull horizontal wire down as far as it will go and cut it in the middle with pliers. Straighten out the kinks. 2. With pliers, form a small hook on each of the two ends. This hanger will be strong enough to hold a small pot or basket. 3. If a third wire is required to strengthen the hanger for larger containers, cut a second coathanger and attach securely near the top of the pot hanger. Make a hook at the other end. To finish, the pot hanger can be painted.
Stella Hutchison, Dalkeith, WA

Hang up

An octopus strap (which holds luggage on trollies) can be used to hang plants up. You can also use them to hang things up in the garden shed.
M Jones
Tweed
Heads
South, NSW

Spice seeder

Use a mixed spice container to plant small seeds. It has pouring and sprinkling sections and so is quite versatile.
Shirley Evans, Boorowa, NSW

Hose sprinkler

A sprinkler can be made from an old watering can rose on the end of your hose.

*Ann McClymont
Longreach, Qld*

Water distiller

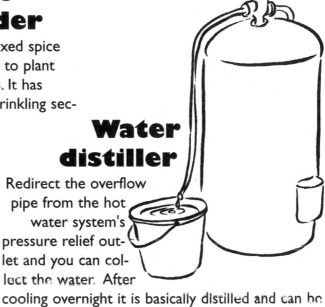

Redirect the overflow pipe from the hot water system's pressure relief outlet and you can collect the water. After cooling overnight it is basically distilled and can be used on the garden.
Geoff Stewart, Bayswater, NSW

Catch those wasps

Mix a potion of honey, meat and an insect poison. Place in an ice-cream container with the lid on and have a ring of 10mm holes around the rim of the container and surround and cover with bricks to prevent animals from getting into the concoction.
*Greg Collins
Dandenong, Vic*

Handy scoop

Cut a hole in a big plastic bottle as shown for carrying compost, or lime for soil amendment. It makes the ingredients easy to access with a hand trowel.
*Mark Hitchins
Cranbourne, Vic*

Side cutter

Side cutting pliers are very effective in pruning vines like honeysuckle. They are a cheap alternative to secateurs—and you don't have to squeeze against a spring.

Doug Gormley, Coolangatta, NSW

Second chance

Buy a bunch of spring onions. Put them in a pail of cold water overnight, leaving the roots intact. In the morning, cut off the spindly tops of the spring onions to the white line. Plant them out in the garden. You will find they grow again very successfully.

Robyn Beth
Parkville, NSW

Hose helper

If you have trouble refilling the oil or fuel on your lawnmower, fit a piece of garden hose on the end of the funnel.

Allon Hofmann
Toowoomba, Qld

Fruit catcher

Here's a simple tool for getting fruit in high places. Cut a plastic container as shown with a 'V' to cut the stalk and the fruit will fall safely into the holder, which is stuck onto a broomstick.

Gordon Winter, Greenwood, WA

Mossie suicide

Fill some ice-cream containers with water and place around the garden. When the mosquito larvae appear, empty in a dry part of the garden. Refill container with water. You interrupt the mozzies' life cycle and have fewer of them in the garden.
Norman Robinson
Ballina, NSW

Keeping in touch

Attach an old shoelace to the watering can's sprayhead and spout using liquid nails. This way you never lose the sprayhead.
D A Mudge, Davoren Park, SA

Plant guard

An easy-to-make plant protector can be salvaged from used plastic honey containers. Make a cut and then use scissors to cut the edges.
Geoff Lott
Kenmore, Qld

Sticking in the knife

From local op shops buy half a dozen old kitchen table/steak knives with wooden handles. Then either paint or electrical tape the handles in bright colours for easy finding, red or yellow, etc., then leave them scattered around the vegie garden beds. Then there is no need to rush back for a knife if you spot the odd zuchinni you have missed, also great for a quick weed of the carrots, etc.
Helen McPhie
Caramut, Vic

Bird feeder

Here's a plastic-bottle bird feeder. Cut as shown.
Daphne Brown
Queanbeyan, NSW

Pest smoker

Boil tobacco up and let it cool. Strain it and then spray it on the tomatoes and fruit trees. This keeps grubs off.
William Allan
Waratah, Tas

Potted peas

Grow sweetpeas from a pot by tying three stakes into a tee-pee shape. Wind garden twine around the stakes to the top of the tripod. This prevents the peas from twining together in a bunch and they grow straight up.
Sharon McCarty
Kallaroo, WA

Quick rot

Store grass clippings in stand-up garbage bags. Put a few holes in the bottom and after a few months the grass will rot down to about a third and may be put on gardens or in worm farms or compost bins to mix with other material. The bags can be used two or three times before the plastic becomes brittle.
Peter Beames
Arcadia Vale, NSW

Bird bagger

Place plastic shopping bags around seedlings to protect them from the blackbirds. Just slit along the bottom of the bag, put it around the seedling and peg in position with three little sticks to hold the bag in place. The bag can act as a warming zone for the roots to snuggle under.
Nancy Brooks, Warragul, Vic

Goodness from the sea

Collect seaweed that has been washed up on to the rocks by the high tide. At home wash the salt off with the hose. Put seaweed into a shopping bag and leave in the sun to decompose. After two or three months, when it's soft and sqashy, put half a spadeful in the watering can. Fill can with water and leave again for about a week. Water sparingly around plants and shrubs. Hose well afterwards. This fer-tiliser is particularly good for tomatoes.

Barbara Maxwell, Gerringong, NSW

Bird haven

Fill a hanging basket with sand, rocks, etc., and place saucer on top. Fill with seed for birds and hang in the tree. To help stop seed getting wet wedge an old esky lid half way down the basket chains.
Karen Erler
Orchard Hills, NSW

Orchids from cuttings

Put cuttings in a tin of very sandy soil. Water until they start spreading roots. Using dried coconut fibre, pull all the stringy fibre off the inside and soak it in a bucket of water. The wet fibre is taken from the water and packed up around the roots of the orchids. Tie around the orchid with string, then tie them to the fence and drench them twice a day until they start shooting. No fertiliser or soil is ever used.
S Ramires, Bohol, Philippines

Corn cob handles

Use the corn cob from after dinner. Let it dry out for a week. Then it becomes a superb handle for files. They last up to two years. The rough outside is a good grip and the core of the cob holds the handle well.
Graham Swift
Port Stephens Shire, NSW

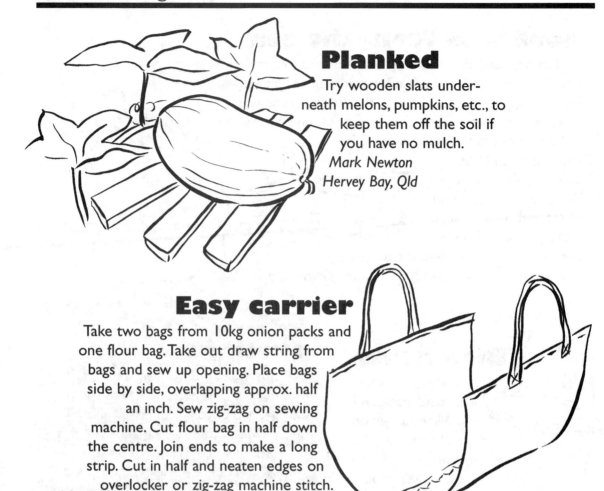

Planked

Try wooden slats under-
neath melons, pumpkins, etc., to
keep them off the soil if
you have no mulch.
Mark Newton
Hervey Bay, Qld

Easy carrier

Take two bags from 10kg onion packs and
one flour bag. Take out draw string from
bags and sew up opening. Place bags
side by side, overlapping approx. half
an inch. Sew zig-zag on sewing
machine. Cut flour bag in half down
the centre. Join ends to make a long
strip. Cut in half and neaten edges on
overlocker or zig-zag machine stitch.
These are the handles. Sew handles to each
end of onion bags. This is a wonderful, no-cost
carrier. It holds so much and has no weight in itself.
Susanne Nixon, Sandy Bay, Tas

A 'tyred' and true garden plan

Make large garden beds of tyres laid out flat in a preplanned shape. The tyre bed
can be surrounded by large stones or smaller ones jammed between each tyre and
the section showing painted, or use a concrete border. Old newspapers may be
stuffed into the tyres as well before covering. Shrubs and plants need to be planted
before covering with chips, hay, etc. Tyre beds keep moist longer due to water
trapped in the tyres.
Toni Greene, Montville, Qld

Instant water

For an instant watering can, get a plastic juice bottle with a hollow handle. Cut the handle at the top end and bend back to form a spout. Block the top opening, fill with water and pour.
Emily Giblin, Battery Point, Tas

Weed hacker

A hacksaw blade tied to a short pole as shown makes a great weeder.
John & Ken Lambkin
Belmont, NSW

Shady protection

I cut some shadecloth into 30cm squares and folded it twice, then cut the corner out to make a hole in the centre of about 8cm diameter and cut up one side to the hole. Place each square under a strawberry plant and fold it around the plant like a collar. It doesn't stop water penetration and it helps to repel weeds and keeps fruit clean.
Harry Simmons, Ormiston, Qld

Looped

Make a wire loop out of heavy wire as shown and embed it in a slot cut through the end of a heavy dowel. Tie off tightly with wire and you have a versatile fruit picker.
David Gilet

Punnet steps

This is an idea for anyone that wants to put a stepping stone track to somewhere. We had some punnet trays, the big ones, so cut the bottoms out, laid them in a hole we dug and filled them up with cement about a step apart. Very handy for the compost bin also.
Henry Williams, Leongatha, Vic

Bulb basket

Old clothes baskets are excellent for growing herbs and bulbs in.
Jean Watson, Hornsby, NSW

Hot stuff

Buy cheap black pepper and scatter this liberally between the plants. This keeps blackbirds from uprooting your seeds.
Betty Mitchell Glenroy, SA

Pipe dreams

Dig a hole and place a piece of plastic pipe about 15cm long vertically into it. Replace the earth to hold the pipe upright. Then, using a funnel, spoon snail pellets into the pipe. The pellets fall to the bottom and well out of pets reach.
J A Jahir, Stratton, WA

Prawns for blowies

To get rid of blowflies, put out six jam jars with metal lids. Fill two-thirds full with water and pop three prawn heads in each. Make three holes in each lid and the flies are almost queuing up to get inside and drown.
J A Jahir, Stratton, WA

Portable potter

For a portable potting tray that fits over the wheelbarrow, stand pots on frame with potting mix in the barrow. Any excess mix falls back into the barrow.
David Lewis, Crows Nest, NSW

Shock absorber

To fix tool heads to handles, use an old motor tube cut into long strips. Stretch it as tight as you can over the end of the handle. Use more rubber strips to bind the stretched strips to the narrow part of the handle. Use two such strips at right angles to each other. Slip the tool head over the rubber strips and thump it down as tight as you can. Then cut away the excess rubber. The rest of the rubber contracts into the space between the head and handle. The rubber grips the head tightly and takes up shrinkage in the timber handle. It also acts as a shock absorber.

Lindsay Corben, Richmond Hill, Tas

Layered slots

A simple method of layering plants is shown here. Cut slots in a plastic box. Wedge in the branch and cover with soil.

Byron Guest, Sawyers Valley, WA

Long reach

I've always had a problem in watering plants like lettuce and broccoli. Either I've got to flood the whole area or walk on newly dug soil to reach the plants. I've solved the problem by using 20mm electrical plastic conduit about 2.5m long. By inserting my watering hose into the big end of the conduit, I can adjust the flow, placing the end next to the plant and water the vegies with ease and comfort without having to walk on any soil.

Nancy Smith, Campbellfield, Vic

Hangup

Keep your gumboots high and dry—and insectproof with trouser hangers.

*Joy Dickson
Ashby, NSW*

Tree lopper

A handy tree pruner made by bolting a hacksaw to a pole.
O Meddings
Belgrave, Vic

Seed store

When I receive a business-size envelope I open it by cutting off one of the side ends. I then use the envelope to store dry seeds in.
Keith Vanstan, Delacombe, Vic

Seedling knife

Use a grapefruit knife to remove seedlings from their little 'cells' in multicellular punnets. They are usually rather fiddly to remove, but with the knife they come out effortlessly without disturbing the roots.
Dorothy Zeylemaker
Toowoomba, Qld

Sharp touch

For maintenance of the garden shovel and spade, and to ensure much quicker and easier digging, you can put a sharp edge on these tools by using a small mill file. Be sure to stroke the file toward the tool's cutting edge. If the shovel or spade is rusty, remove the rust with a wire brush before using the file.
Paula Peach, Strawberry Hills, NSW

Strung along

Use a 20x10x1cm piece of plywood; two 5cm bullet-head nails in the middle to hold while unwinding and the same each side, offset, for rewinding. I tie a loop on the end of the string to slip over a small stake. The 'V' is used as a stop against a stake at the other end. No need to tie it—just pull the line taut and form the 'V' against the stake.
Bob Lee, Charlton, Qld

Rat-proof compost

Rats and mice burrow underneath the compost bin. Buy some blind wire, cut it slightly bigger than the base of the bin, thread wire around the outside of the bird wire, put the compost bin on top and gently pull the wire tight. It is easy to pull a bit of wire and twist, then move around the bin and do it again and again so the friction of the wire doesn't break the bird wire. The whole job takes about half an hour and works brilliantly—no rats!

Ravena Thompson, Mapleton, Qld

Hose holder

Take a bundle of old coathangers and cut off both ends about 15cm from the tip. This leaves you with a handy piece of wire, like an inverted 'V'. Turn it over and place it over the hose pipe, pressing it into the soil until it is holding the hose firmly in place.

Nicolette Quekett, Fremantle, WA

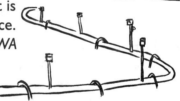

Herbal help

I don't want to use insecticide sprays when making compost and risk killing off the earthworms. Now I add small, crushed cuttings of some or all of the following after each addition of vegetable matter: lavender, lemon grass, rosemary, scented geranium, peppermint, tansy and penny royal. The strong scents of these plants have successfully deterred undesirable insects.

Muriel Kilian, Riverton, SA

Tyre guard

A hacksaw blade slotted and tied into a piece of wood makes cutting old tyres easy.

Anon, Maleny, Qld

Cool home for worms

Drill several holes in the back of an old fridge. Lay it on its back off the ground on a small platform. Half fill with old manure or cardboard and start putting kitchen scraps, waste paper, old clothing and a few hundred tiger worms inside. Collect the juice underneath in tins and within three months you will have castings available for the garden. Leave fridge door slightly ajar and you could have a frog habitat too.
Chris Pogasse, Tanja, NSW

Tree protection

To protect tree trunks from mulch. Take a strip of gutter guard and cut to a length a little longer than the tree circumference. Join ends together by threading coathanger wire vertically through the holes, allowing extra wire to be pushed into the ground. The top may be bent over to avoid injury. A second wire can be added on the other side to secure if necessary.
Siddie Reader, Westbury, Tas

Magpie reflections

Magpies in attack mode can be easily deflected or confused. Glue pieces of mirror or anything reflective, to your hat . The birds keep away.
*Maureen Wilson
Gympie, Qld*

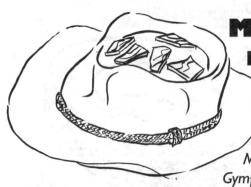

Racked

A quick and easy boot rack can be made from a brick and a couple of dowels.
*Jimmy &
Freda Watson
Blackmans Bay, Tas*

Deadly brew

Last year I hung soft-drink bottles half full of beer in every fruit tree, with small holes in the top of the bottle. I got very few fruit fly and every bottle nearly filled with dead ones.
*Di Thompson
North Star
NSW*

Dog heaven

For gardeners who love their dogs, in autumn when the Japanese maple leaves are dry and crunchy on the ground, scoop them up into hessian bags (size depends on the size of the dog)—about 3/4 or loosely fill the bag—and either tie or stitch it closed. Make up a few of these bags and they make absolutely splendid beds for dogs during the winter—they are soft and warm. At the end of winter you can recycle the leaves back onto the garden as mulch.
Muriel Stuart, Bowral, NSW

Get the scoop

Make a scoop for getting blood and bone, potting mix, etc., out of the bag by using a piece of 10cm diameter PVC pipe about 30cm long, a piece of round koppers log 10cm diameter, a wooden file handle, a long wood screw and four flat-head galvanised nails.
Brian Mason, Nambucca Heads, NSW

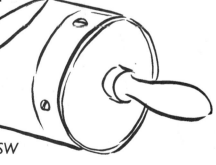

Seed raiser

Use milk or plastic juice bottles for raising lettuce, bean and pumpkin seeds. Cut a fair way up the bottle neck (lid taken off). Fill the bottle neck with soil. Put seeds in the soil. Fill bottom of the bottle with water. Sit neck top down into the water. Once seeds start growing well you will get excellent root systems in the water. When ready to plant, squeeze the neck, tip upside down and the plant easily comes out.
Camilla Whishaw, Carrick, Tas

Ant attack

Sprinkle talcum powder liberally over the nests of black ants. Two or three applications are sometimes necessary. This ploy is successful without using chemicals.
*Isobel Evans
Blackheath, NSW*

Tasty pulp

Thinly spread very wet paper pulp directly onto the garden and cover with pea straw. Keep fairly wet for a few days. Soon there is no trace of the paper pulp and no objections from the worms!
Ivy Kenneady, White Cliffs, NSW

A new bent

Take a thickish coathanger. Cut the twisted bits off and straighten about 75cm of it. Place the middle round the slot in your plastic hose rose and bend the wire tightly half a turn so the two ends are parallel. Next, take it off the rose and clamp it in a vice so that the two ends stick up in the air with about the two inches or so that goes round the hose in the vice. Bend the two ends towards you as far as you can, keeping them parallel. Now take it out of the vice and continue bending both ends to get the full U-turn and you have the complete holder.
Derek Broadbent, Clontarf, NSW

Quick bird feeder

Use two plastic saucers approximately 20cm across; a 15cm plastic pot with drainage holes, on the sides not underneath; and half of a second 15cm pot to keep the lid in place. The pots are glued to the lids, holes drilled through the centres with a heated wire. A cord with a knot underneath holds the lot together and the top of the cord is tied to the branch of a tree.

Dini Belgraver
Armadale, Vic

Tap turner

Bending to turn taps in the watering system can be difficult. I made an extension tube out of 25mm grey electrical conduit. Cut twice across the base and any length and a cross-piece in the top for extra twist.

Phil Craig
Heathmont, Vic

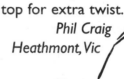

Big hands

You need a board about 15x20cm. Nail a piece of leather onto this. Insert the fingers of a glove under the leather, keeping the thumb on top. Make another for the other hand. These 'extended hands' are very handy for picking up leaves and weeds.

I Karuty
Belmont, NSW

Cannibals

Snails and slugs love to feed on their own freshly killed relatives. At night crush the snails and slugs, and place a small amount of snail bait on the dead pests. In the morning you will find several more dead pests.

Jack Feney, Willagee, WA

Shiny solution

To get rid of aphids on roses, put some water in a spray container and add a good dollop of vegetable cooking oil. Sprayed on the roses, this gets rid of the aphids and puts a lovely shine on the leaves. It doesn't hurt the plant either.

Mary McGregor
Padbury, WA

Knit one

Use old knitting needles with seed packets to mark the area.
Edna Couper, Doveton, Vic

Seed raiser

Cut a two-litre fruit juice bottle as shown with a Stanley knife to form a lid. Open the lid and place the punnet, with seeds already sown, inside and then close it. The neck of the bottle will serve as a convenient grip for handling. When the seedlings appear, place a pencil-size stick under the lid to afford ventilation. Allow the plants to reach the level of the lid before taking them out to harden prior to transplanting.
Brian Shaddock, Burnie, Tas

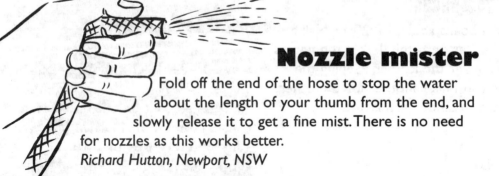

Nozzle mister

Fold off the end of the hose to stop the water about the length of your thumb from the end, and slowly release it to get a fine mist. There is no need for nozzles as this works better.
Richard Hutton, Newport, NSW

Overhead sprinkler

For overhead watering, place a tomato stake at strategic (but inconspicuous) positions in the shrubbery. When it's time for watering slip a length of 4cm pipe (a few inches longer than the stake) over the stake and, into the top of this, position a spiked sprinkler. These sprinklers retail for around $4.00 and can of course be used also in the ground as intended.
Sylvia Brown, Fig Tree, NSW

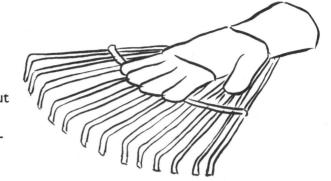

Glove rake

Glue an old pair of welding gloves to a couple of old lawn rake heads. If glued at the correct angle (around 45 degrees) then the rake heads are just like a gigantic pair of hands. Putting garden waste like leaves and grass clippings into the wheelbarrow has never been easier.
John Simpson, Lara, Vic

Design trick

When laying out garden designs on existing lawn areas, there is a quick and easy way to see your finished layout before you start. I first mow the lawn areas to be retained on a very short setting. Then mow the lawn in the proposed garden areas on a much higher setting. You can easily see results and it is easy to change. It is easy to plan and place pots around to see which trees need to be moved. You can visualise the end result and see if it is really practical.
Louise Oakley
Pascoe Vale, Vic

Tap turner

A small item for backyard taps that are too tight to turn on and off when you have arthritis in your hands. Use 15cm of electrician's conduit (20mm) or similar. Drill a 10mm hole 10cm from one end and cut a slot out with a hacksaw blade. Slide this over the tap when you want to turn the handle on or off, it takes the pressure off the hand and is better than other items we have tried.
Paul Bowman, Sanctuary Point, NSW

Tong transplanter

For a simple variation of a commercial seedling transplanter, use kitchen serving tongs. Just push the ends into the soil around the seedling, squeeze tight and lift out, then push into the soil in the appointed place and release pressure on the tongs and withdraw. It allows good positioning of the seedling with minimum disturbance of the root system.

Jim Pratt, Warragul, Vic

Curly cure 1

Several years ago I planted a miniature peach tree, it was covered in curly leaf for two seasons. I planted some oregano seeds and now the curly leaf has completely disappeared.
Frances Burke, Wynyard, Tas

Curly cure 2

This is how we stopped leaf curl on our nectarine tree. We let the 'marshmallow' weed grow in our backyard and then cut long stems and placed them across the branches of the fruit tree, we did this at the first sign of life in the tree.
Bet Loechel, Lucindale, SA

Backache saver

All you need is a leaf rake (metal ones are best) and a 50-litre (rectangular) plastic bin. Rake the leaves into a pile and place the bin on its side with the opening facing the leaves. Stand with one foot beside the bin and one foot behind. Rake the leaves into the bin (keeping your back straight). When the box seems full, tip it onto its back using the rake (the rake also stops the leaves from falling out). Now pack the leaves down with one foot, still standing up straight. It will only be half full after this step. Put the rake over the box and tip it on its side again (the rake stops leaves from falling out). Take up the same position as you started with and rake more leaves into the bin. When the bin seems full, tip it onto its back just as you did before. Now you can bend your knees keeping your back straight to pick up the bin. The leaves are easier to handle in this compressed form, allowing you to tip them onto the compost heap, drop them through the mulcher, hook a plastic bag under the bin's rim, and tip the leaves into the bag.
Robert Grantham, Doncaster, Vic

Plant hat

Cut through a two-litre drink bottle. Also cut four holes in the bottom of the base. Stick a skewer on the top of each of the corners of the base. Stick the funnel-shaped piece to the skewers. Put some soil in the bottom of the holder and plant seedlings or a potplant in the soil. Water through the top of the holder or in between the skewers.

Anna Greble, Inglewood, WA

Rot stop

Slit the side of a pot and remove the bottom. This goes around the tree or shrub and when you lay thick mulch down it keeps the mulch away and prevents collar rot.

Tom Lynch, Alderley, Qld

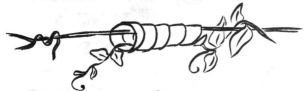

Creepers!

After planting a creeping snail plant I wanted to train it along wires on my patio. I found it a chore using plastic-covered ties. I came up with a simple idea that you may like. Cut a continuous diagonal through a plastic tube. It's easy to apply, can be used anywhere along a wire and expands as the plant grows thicker.

Peter McOnegal, Brighton, Qld

Birdbath

Plastic rubbish bin lids can be very good bird baths, supported upside down on an old tyre. Cut three equidistant holes in the wall on one side (or burn with soldering iron). Drive three lengths of old water pipe or angle iron or long

lasting stakes into the ground, to match the holes. See there is greenery close by where birds can feel safe, perch, preen, rest or wail. Set the tyre horizontally on the stakes, hammer if necessary (through the tyre) to get the tyre level. Set the plastic lid on the tyre and fill with water. It is easy to clean. I have two of these bird baths used regularly for ten years. Sparrows, starlings, wrens, little wattle birds, goldfinches, several varieties of honey eaters, butcher birds, blackbirds, silver eyes are some we watch.

Ken Blackwell, South Arm, Tas

Mini greenhouse

A simple mini greenhouse can be made with half an egg carton and a plastic drink bottle with its neck cut off.
Dennis C Hazel
Pambula, NSW

Seal & deliver

Cut a security seal from a two-litre soft drink bottle. They are very useful to secure plants to canes and saves tying. There is enough tension left in the plastic to stop them falling off.
Harry Medlycott, Reynella, SA

Ring 'em

I have come up with a very simple idea for those plant labels. I have bought a very large ring from the newsagency. I then punched a hole in each label with a hole punch and put them on the ring. Now I find it easy to look up plants that have worked well and those that haven't worked so well. It looks a bit like this.
Rose Gooding, Warburton, Vic

Thumb saver

Guide stakes with a section of polypipe as you hit them into the ground.

Ted Standfield
McLaren Vale, SA

Portable shed

Others might be interested in the barrow my husband created for me. We live on two hectares and frequently I would be at the furthermost point from the tool-shed and desperately need my loppers or the rake or some other item I'd failed to bring with me. This creation is lightweight. The green bins can be used to carry extras for whatever job I might be doing. When filled with prunings or weeds it can be easily lifted off to be emptied. The little white bucket holds my bottle of drinking water, sunglasses, sunscreen and hat. The red bin is divided for the various tools, trowel, fork, weeder, etc. The length of plumbing pipe on the side holds the rake, hoe or other similar tools and the two vertical pipes carry the heavier loppers and shears.

Elizabeth Simonsen, Curlewis, Vic

Curly cure 3

Fruit trees with curly leaf don't need to be sprayed. Dig out roots and all of one dock weed and hang it in your tree, and the curly leaf will disappear in about two weeks. I've used this method also with rose bushes and now haven't any black spot or aphids.
Carl Retusen, Kerang, Vic

Staked

Where you have to support riser stems but don't have a secure post to attach them to, use garden stakes.
*Michael Todd
Cannon Vale, NSW*

Lattice arch

Get a bit of plastic lattice, an off-cut, bend it over your seed box and put the whole lot into a plastic shopping bag. It works so well that you have to be careful not to get spindly seedlings.
Dave Jackson, Coombabah, Qld

Heavy holder

To make a snail bait holder, use a four-litre and a two-litre ice-cream container, approx. 40cm of 30cm O/D PVC pipe, two 8cm lengths of 30cm pipe. Cut a hole in centre of each side of containers just below ridge of flange. Place two-litre container inside four-litre container and push long pipe through each container. Likewise push smaller pipes through other two sides. Centre the containers and fill space between with a sloppy mix of cement, when completely dry, pipes can be removed by screwing round and carefully withdrawing, container can then be sealed and painted. When finished a bait tray can be placed underneath. Finished job is heavy enough to stop animals, wind and birds (and the average child) from turning it over. Out of the weather bait lasts until eaten by snails and is not wasted.

Jack Brabham, Loch Sport, Vic

Wasp trap

This is a good way of trapping European wasps, using a two-litre soft drink bottle and a thick honey, sugar, bread and water mix. Simply cut the bottle so the neck fits neatly inside of bottom section (leave about 3/4 of bottom section). Pour honey solution into bottom section. Insert top section spout down. Wasps fly in and can't get out.

Paul Prestiney, Pearsondale, Vic

Knee saver

A knee and elbow saver, especially for arthritis sufferers can be made up of wastes, as a double-sided general-purpose seat for such jobs as gardening, tiling, floor sanding and low wall painting, etc. It avoids the use of elbow and knee guards (and surface scratching). Use a four-litre paint tin and inexpensive rubber based carpet. Adhesion of these components is either a liquid or pressure-gun glue.

Clive Martin
Hyams Beach, NSW

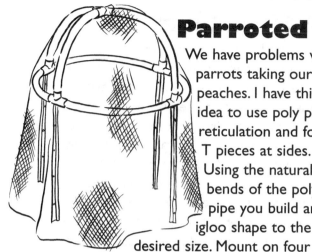

Parroted

We have problems with parrots taking our peaches. I have this idea to use poly pipe reticulation and four T pieces at sides. Using the natural bends of the poly pipe you build an igloo shape to the desired size. Mount on four star pickets and cover with bird netting, allowing room for the tree to grow.
Dave Frost, Leschenault, WA

Seed strips

Take a single white tissue and cut it lengthwise into two strips. Fold each strip longways and open it out again, leaving a definite fold visible. Make a small trench along the seed-raising mix and place the prepared tissues along the trench overlapping them slightly until the desired length is obtained. Using a mist spray, slightly dampen the tissues. Then carefully place the seeds along the fold in the white tissues at the correct spacing. They are easy to see and if necessary may be thinned with tweezers. Cover with seed raising mix to specified depth and water lightly. You will find that, as the seeds germinate, the tiny roots will pierce the soft wet paper and by the time comes for planting out the tissue will have completely disintegrated.
Jim Pashley, Falcon, WA

Dripper

I have used this idea for years, and have found it most successful when planting out seedlings, placing a bottle by each plant, creating a gentle flood area directly on the root area. According to need, a different sized hole will give different flow rates. I sometimes use the flat head of a three-inch nail, or maybe the pointed end for a finer hole. I hold the nail with pliers in a gas flame till red hot, then jab it into the desired spot on the PET bottle. I find that the recessed part of the bottom flutes will give an angle just right for the drip. If it does not work at first, wait till the sun hits it, or a gentle tap will set it off. After losing a clutch of quail chicks because they could not reach their water dish on hatching out, I now leave a bottle such as this, with a fine hole for them to lick a drip as required. Also, a bottle hung by twisting wire around the neck can serve as an overhead dripper, to start plants off.
Ian & Glad McCulloch
Elizabeth Downs, SA

Self waterers

We have been using variations of milk cartons for seed trays in our small commercial nursery. There are several possibilities with this, such as semi-hydroponic or self-watering or complete drain but no spill by not perforating the outer carton half or perforate both and let the water drain. Take an empty cardboard milk carton and cut it completely in half lengthwise. Take the side that has not been the pouring side and use this as a base. Then cut some drain holes in the edge of the other side. Cut drain holes—as many as you want—on the lower sides of the tray you are inserting by placing some sticks in the base of the outer half. It is possible to sit the seed tray above the drained water if this is what you require.

Chris Lockyer, Blairgowrie, Vic

Strung out

Do not plant seeds in a drill but stretch a line, in which has been tied evenly spaced knots, from one end of the desired location to mark the line of the drill. Seed packets note the distance between plants after thinning so the seeds are placed at this distance apart. I usually use polyester venetian blind cord for my lines and tie the knots 15cm apart. Polyester withstands ultraviolet light very well so the lines can be left out in all weather, some of my lines are over 20 years old. Leave the lines in place until the seeds are through and hoeing is quite safe, since you know where your seeds are. There is still some thinning to be done but it is only a matter of removing say 50–60% instead of the usual 90–99% in a normal drill.

Antony Clarke, Chifley, ACT

Seedling hat

To care for seedlings during hot summers, I keep my empty 1kg yoghurt containers and cut the bottom like a windmill, removing every second vane and the tips of those remaining. I then put these over my seedlings and put a small bamboo stake in to hold the container in place. Pushing the container into the soil also kept snails away while the plant got established. I found this allowed a certain amount of sun in so that the plants did not grow tender and you could water easily.

Freda Little, Bowral, NSW

Freesia crutch

The huge new freesias that have the long stems I find flop over. I planted mine last year in several pots under an upturned wire basket. This provided great support for the stems and trained them into a nicely arranged pot. When in bud I nestled the pot amidst other small growing plants such as agathea. The pot was hidden and the freesias bloomed beautifully, looking as if they had always been planted there.
Brenda Garde, Lalor Park, NSW

Curtains for the birds

To stop birds from picking seedlings, use some old net curtains, put a stick in the middle of the boxes, curtains tucked around.
Barbara McLeod Kuttabul, Qld

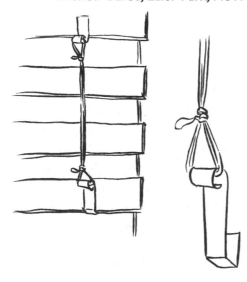

Hangers on

I would like to pass on an easily made gadget for a wet day. I have made many of these cutting strips of thin galvanised iron (old roofing flashing cut-offs etc.) 4cm wide. I bend them to shape with a pair of ordinary combination pliers and cut them with tinsnips or old scissors, they can be used on paling, picket or wire fences. I use old pantyhose for tying back many vegies and plants to these clips.
John Hambling, Newtown, Vic

Thinning carrots made easy

I hate to thin carrots and this occurred to me while soaking a batch of other seeds. Take a large flat tray (I use my baking trays). Cover with sheets of paper towel, wet, then, while having a cup of tea, I sit the trays on my lap and spread the seeds to the required growing distance. It takes very little effort and is very relaxing. Then slide the wet sheets off the tray directly onto the prepared bed.
Lucia Williamson, Research, Vic

Weeping frame

A frame for a weeping standard can be made from a wire basket and a stake. Two wire baskets can make a ball-on-a-stick frame. A sprinkler tube can be run up the stake. Join the baskets and their rims and fix with wire. Balance on top of a stake and fix.

Jay Bourke, Eagle Heights, Qld

Bird lure

A nest to bring native birds to your garden can be made from old plastic pot planters.

*Bob Johnstone
Moorooduc,
Vic*

Hidden water

We have recently put all our potplants on our patio on to the automatic reticulation system using 13mm polypipe. Originally we had 4mm polypipe feeder lines coming from the main pipe in the garden, over the outside of the pot into the pot with a dripper on the end. This looked rather messy, not to mention that the black polypipe heated up during the day. We didn't want anything permanent as we may want to move the pots some time.

To solve this problem what we did was to put a piece of black 13mm polypipe into the pot, going from one of the drainage holes (assuming these are larger than 13mm) at the bottom to the surface of the soil. Then, by sitting the pots on some feet (leaving a gap between the bottom of the pot and the ground), you can thread the 4mm polypipe, from the main pipe, up the 13mm pipe onto the top of the soil and then screw in your end fitting. By doing this there is no unsightly black pipe coming up the outside of your nice pots and you can swap plants around on your patio without the need to repot the polypipe again.

Renae & Eric Bastholm, Kiara, WA

80

Easy rider

Put post in ground, fix bike wheel to top. Hang string or wire from wheel to stake in ground. Perfect for peas, beans (runner) or sweet peas. Also ideal for shed with hooks to hang tools or paintbrushes.

Don Gregory
Loganlea, Qld

Meltdown

Store grass clippings in stand-up garbage bags. Put a few holes in the bottom and after a few months the grass will decompose down to about a third. The bags can be used two to three times before they become brittle.

Peter Beames
Arcadia Vale, NSW

Doggone

There's nowt worse than stepping in a barker's egg (also known as dog sh_t) whilst you are out enjoying the garden. But using my exclusive barker's egg remover you can once again venture barefoot into the garden with confidence. All you need is a plastic two-litre drink container (rectangular in cross-section). I use a cordial bottle and cut through three sides as shown (leaving the fourth side as a hinge). To use, open bottle, place one side flat on the grass/soil etc next to the offending barker's egg, then close top and flick barker's egg to the bottom of the bottle and open bottle again ready for the next egg.

Paul Sellers, Hazelmere, WA

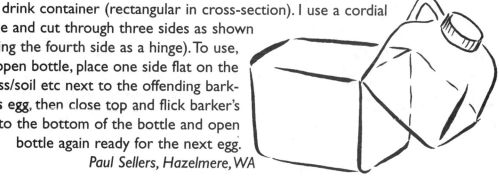

A new fashion statement

I use an old woollen beanie to line a wire hanging basket and found it effective, durable and good looking. It also has the advantage that the fibres are not pulled out and used as nesting material by the local birds. As this is so successful, I now cut up and use my old woollen pullovers as basket liners. I have so far confined my colour schemes to grey and green but, depending on a gardener's style and taste, the liners could conceivably be used to brighten a dull garden or patio.

Michael Cunningham, Hackham, SA

Spoken for

A handy storage holder can be made from a bicycle wheel hung up on a wall. Each season I use at least 15 bags of potting mix and when empty I place the empty bags between the spokes until required later (for dumping rubbish etc). Fold empty bags in rolls and stick between spokes. The bags will expand and will be held.

Colin Mannering, Altona, Vic

Corn care

Place old sweetcorn canes thickly between the strawberry rows in autumn. They seem to take about 12 months to rot and are useful for keeping fruit off the ground and acting as mulch. It's cheap, gets rid of the canes, allows air to circulate a bit and keeps the strawberries clean for picking.

K Matthews
Westbury, Tas

A breeze

Whenever we sow a new lawn or repair a patch of old, we deter the birds by using a group of toy windmills. One per square metre or so poked into the soil with the windmill parts in a variety of directions seems to work. It only takes a slight breeze to make them spin and the birds seem to dislike them. They are inexpensive and available from anywhere you'd buy kids' party paraphernalia.

Margot McDonald, Elwood, Vic

Shady tidy carrier

You need a piece of shadecloth about 1.5 x .75m and a piece of rope about 6m long. Make a hem along each side of the shadecloth, about 3cm in width. Thread the rope through one side then back down the other side. All you have to do is place the cuttings or whatever across the cloth, then when you have a big bundle simply pull up the loop rope over the bundle put the other end of the rope through the loop and pull tight.

Les & Penny Marshall, Nambour, Qld

Windowbox

With an old car windscreen and bricks, build an area the size of the windscreen by stacking layers of old bricks and stones for the four walls. Place the windscreen on top of the brick/stone work. The brick/stonework can be raised by adding more bricks and stones to existing walls as the seedlings grow. Lift the windscreen during watering of seedlings and cover again. Deters birds, possums and dogs.

Su Thong, Glen Waverley, Vic

Sweeper

Here's a sweeper-upper for people with a bad back. Use an old meat tin cut one side off and screw a long handle on the other side.

*Elizabeth Hastings
Dee Why, NSW*

Getting to grips with tool handles

To permanently affix the handle of any gardening tool, use high-strength epoxy two-part glue. The first thing to remember is that the glue is stronger than the paint on the inside of the metal part, so deeply scratch the inside beneath the paint in a crosshatch way. The wooden handle should only be an easy push fit, again scored in the same way. When this is done, smear both surfaces thoroughly with the well-mixed glue and bring them together in a twisting motion, then gently twist them to and fro making certain that the glue is evenly spread; finally a light tap in and the job is done. Leave for a week to cure.

Sydney Taylor, Gladstone, Qld

Knotty grip

Further to the 'hose pulling on tap' problem. Use a prussik loop, a simple device used by absell-ers to climb up a rope, as the prussik knot slips when not under lead and tightens when it is not.

Anon, Goulburn, NSW

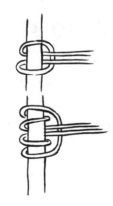

Well netted

Those little red and green net bags that come around fruit can be used as little plant protectors over and around seedlings. They can be laid over sticks around the seedlings. The bigger and thicker ones can be cut into cylinders of the required length and slipped over sticks around the plant.

Maree Ledson, Greenacre, NSW

Cap this

Using an ice-cream container, cut a three-sided hole and bend up from inside. Cut so as to fit snugly on a stake. The container becomes adjustable to any height on the stake.

Colin Taylor, Alexandria, NSW

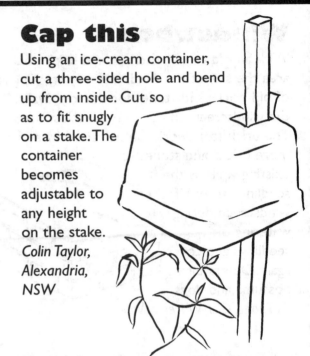

Hanger trellis

Use three hangers for the basic module. Let 'A' slightly overlap 'B' with hooks facing outward. Hanger 'C' can then be slipped over the hooks of 'A' and 'B'. Hook 'C' is then fed through the 'A-B' overlap and the tip fed back over hanger 'B' to lock it in position.

Rod Horsburgh, Mt Mee, Qld

Bagging the potplants

Use empty bread bags for transporting small potplants. Slide them into the bag; make a knot with the top and you have a handy carrier (waterproof as well).

Mrs W Meeuwissen, Daw Park, SA

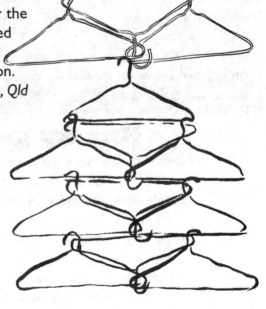

Self-waterer

Two 2-litre ice-cream buckets make a useful self-watering pot. By stacking, the height of the rim creates a space which becomes a reservoir. Drill drainage holes in the base of top bucket then stack with the reservoir bucket. Drill four overflow holes through both buckets while stacked. Drill holes through second rim while stacked to attach wires if a hanging version is required. Bright sunlight will reduce the lifespan of the plastic.
Rod Horsburgh, Mt Mee, Qld

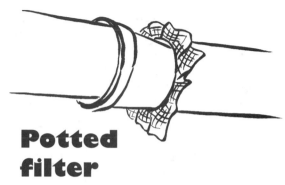

Potted filter

Use plant pots to join drainage pipes together. The base of the pots should be cut off if water flow is excessive. With the help of patches of shade-cloth you can also filter the water.
Dave Fergusson, Warrion, Vic

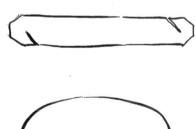

Rooted spuds

You can root rose cuttings by sticking them into a big raw potato.
*Paula Peach
Strawberry Hills, NSW*

Plastic ties

It is easy to make plant ties cut from an old plastic pot. A bottle or ice-cream carton would serve as well. The diagram show how the tie works.
*Betty & Bill Thorpe
Noble Park, Vic*

Meshing in

To support tall-growing flowers, instead of staking each plant try using garden mesh with a 10x10cm grid. The mesh can be cut to the height required . When the plants are around 25 30cm high, run the mesh vertically down both sides of the plants in and around the plants if they are in clumps. To support the mesh, use cheap, thin 90cm bamboo garden canes threaded down through the mesh.
Eddie Johnson, Gwelup, WA

Weedmobile

A kid's cart can make a handy weedmobile, and include a welcome seat.
Audrey Jack, Cronulla, NSW

Stumped

To make a bird bath or feed tray, use a tree stump for the base and the saucer from a large plastic pot for the top.
Robyn Leah, Cessnock, NSW

Labelled

Save all rubber scraper handles (wooden or plastic, as long as they have a hole on one end) and attach the base of a margarine container. Cut them round or heart shaped.
Margaret Brown, Minlaton, SA

Hiding the label

When I plant a rose, azalea or anything I particularly want to remember the name of, I write the name with a black marker pen on the blade of a white plastic knife and stick the blade in the ground up close to the trunk of the plant. By writing the name on the blade its protected from the sun, the handle is unobtrusive and it's dead easy.
Joy Fidock, NSW

Potted hen

When your terracotta pots break, try this for a perfect nest for the hen who lays outdoors! It gives some protection from the rain for when they start sitting.

Aylwen Garden, Yarralumla, ACT

See-through roots

When striking cuttings in water, cut a soft-drink bottle in half and invert the top (funnel-shaped) piece into the bottom half almost filled with water (see diagram). Put cuttings through the hole. This way the roots can be seen forming and the top leaves of the cutting don't get soggy or pollute the water. (You can do basil this way.)

Liz Ahearn, Blacksoil, Qld

Seeper

When garden soil is sandy, cut the bottom of a pot and twist the edge into the sand around the plant, then fill the pot full of water, it then slowly seeps into the soil with very little run-off.

Norm Davies
South Yarra, Vic

Killer news

Use newspaper to kill off grass for the creation of new garden beds. Lay a generous layer over the newly mowed lawn and cover it with leaf litter or lawn clippings. Dig a line around the edge of the paper-covered area and tuck newspaper into this cut. This very effectively prevents grass runners from growing into the newly created garden bed.

Alison Dawes, Dubbo, NSW

Tied up

To use plastic shopping bags to tie up bundles of prunings for the weekly rubbish, cut the bag in half. Put one handle through the other. Bring bottom of second bag through handle and pull.
Ann Rapinett, Dandenong, Vic

Multipurpose pantihose

The body section of the pantihose is great for large pots, the thigh section for 20–23 cm pots and the lower for small pots with the feet making a great drying bag for seeds. Stretch over new seeds. Small stakes can be added as stocking is stretched. Use a kitchen or plant tie for the top. Larger stakes can be added as plants grow by stretching stocking. Tape stake ends so that they don't pierce the net.
Marilyn Harris, Ridgehaven, SA

Stiletto spikes

To aerate the lawn. Instead of using a garden fork, I walk around the lawn wearing an old pair of metal stiletto heels. If you do this while the lawn is still soft from rain, you can aerate the lawn without any exertion or aching arm muscles.
Margaret Benney
Craigieburn, Vic

Spray guide

When you need to spray an individual weed or plant, and you don't want the spray to go onto the plants nearby, use a cut down two-litre plastic milk container as shown.
Pamellia-Ann Abel
Bracken Ridge, Qld

Compost coverup

When applying compost around young plants, place 6" plastic or terracotta pots over them and then throw the compost on whilst the pots protect the plants.
Keith Clark, Fairy Meadow, NSW

Leaf scoop

Form fencing wire into a circle then flatten a third of this (see diagram). Then place a large feed or grain bag inside this frame and sew the open end onto this frame. When it is leaf raking-up time simply lay this on the ground and rake the leaves straight into the bag. The wire frame leaves both hands free to rake.
Val Ireland, Allonah, Tas

Inverted logic

If planting things in a very large container and you want to save soil or reduce weight if plants do not need the whole pot filled with soil, place an inverted plant pot in the container before putting in the soil. This is much lighter than using bricks or rocks. Put a few piece of flat wood under the rim of the smaller pot to allow drainage.
Evelyn Austin
Collie, NSW

Water boots

We have found a use for our old discarded gumboots. They can be used as a container for water plants like water hyacinths and irises.
Noel Carr, Darkes Forest, NSW

Easy walls

Use concrete cylinders as garden/retaining walls. Easy to lay, can bend to the contour required, have excellent drainage, stable, environmentally sound and unlimited life.
Edwin Berzins, Carlingford, NSW

Crimp stopper

To stop the hose crimping, cut the top part of two big flower pots and fit them into the well of the reel, one each way. Then put the hose back on.
Harvey MacLinden
Murray Lakes, SA

Glasshouse

Using a two-litre coke bottle cut the top off and the bottom, then attach both top and bottom together with sticky tape. Now it is a seed tray and mini glasshouse. Just lift the top to water and put it back down for warmth.
Steven Ashwith
Dandenong, Vic

Lime spreader

For spreading anything on your garden that shouldn't be in touch with skin, such as lime, etc., make a shovel scoop by cutting the bottom and one side out of a two-litre bottle.
Julia Wither
Gunnedah, NSW

Watersaver

When running the hot tap for doing the dishes, there's a quantity of cold water preceding the hot. Keep an empty juice bottle on the sink handy to collect this water. At nearly one litre each time this is a substantial amount of water to save for watering plants.

Kevin Saunders, Armidale, NSW

Drip feeder

Drill a small hole (about 2mm) in the side at the bottom of an old bucket and fill it with water and place at the base of a shrub. It delivers the right amount of water directly to the root zone.

*Chris Nilsen,
Sydney, NSW*

Sunshade

Thread two 4m lengths of 2.5cm polythene water pipe through whatever length of shade cloth to cover a garden bed.

*Gavin Shaw
Quirindi, NSW*

Handy scoop

A handy scoop for pellets, manures, etc., can be made by nailing a small tin can onto the end of a piece of wood.

*R Snell,
Malvern, Vic*

Non-wetter

To water without wetting leaves, bury a perforated tin can in the midst of seedlings. It is also a good way to feed liquid fertilisers.

*A George
Dandenong, Vic*

And there's more . . .

Drip & join

The new dripping hoses that are made from recycled car tyres are terrific and a great way to give good deep watering but they are very expensive. To use them, but to cut costs, I place them only where I need them to wet the roots and join the in-between bits with ordinary black poly pipe that is used for drip systems.
Tom Laber, Eltham, Vic

Canned plants

For those plants or shrubs that resent being transplanted, cut both ends out of a suitable sized tin, soak around the plant until soil is soft and press the tin right down, enclosing the plant. Leave for about a week then dig down and slip a sharp spade under the tin and lift and transfer to position you want.
Anon, Oakey, Qld

Daily grind

People who live in units have a problem disposing of vegetable scraps and other similar matter that can provide a good source of nourishment for their pot plants, etc. Simply save such scraps in a plastic bag in the fridge and when these are sufficient blend them in an ordinary food blender. This provides a good and natural liquid fertiliser for potplants.
Bruce Mallowes, Dungog, NSW

Long-distance seeding

My friend has a bad back so when he plants seeds he first makes a hole with the handle of a rake, then using a length of PVC pipe he drops the seed down it while holding the pipe over the hole. The pipe is just a little larger than the hole.
E M Devlin, Busselton, WA

Shady reflections

As we have iron fences we had a lot of trouble with plants being burnt with reflected heat. We put shadecloth on the wooden fence posts and rails.
George Charlton, Tarro, NSW

Snail bends

I have cats and dread them picking up snail/slug killer. I have a piece of plumbing pipe, the sink-width white stuff. Put a right-angle bend between two pieces of pipe about a foot or so long. Put a good bundle of pellets in and shake them into the bend. Put behind a bush-type plant (just so it can't be seen). It will quickly fill with snail shells. Tip out and start again.
Pat Hill, Primrose Sands, Tas

Water levels

When I water the potplants I also fill a glass jar (left amongst the potplants). The level of water in the glass jar lets me

know when it is time to water the plants. If there has been rainfall the jar fills up and I don't over-water my plants.
Roslyn Fowler, Bellevue, WA

Filing shed

In my garden shed I have a broom handle put across the corner roof area and from this I have hung an ordinary shoe bag with pockets that hold lots of gardening needs like seed packets, string for tying plants, small tools, even spray cans. From the broom handle I have clipped on a 'clothes dryer'— the sort with clothes pegs around it. This holds several pairs of gloves, paper clippings, bulb packets, etc.
Eve Hughes, Lithgow, NSW

Manure mulch

I have been using sheep manure on my garden for years. The pellets take an age to break down. I usually put some in my compost bin, but the stuff I use on the garden I put through my mulcher. It

makes an easy-to-use powder that is easily incorporated into the soil and can be used in potting mix as well.
Jan Ebbels, Hawthorn, Qld

Second life

I buy a lot of shallots—the downside is they only last about a week in the fridge. But I have found that when you bring your bunch of shallots home from the store, put them in the garden in full sun. They happily continue to grow in your garden. They seem undeterred by time out of the ground.
Gerry Teekman, New Farm, Qld

Now why don't you . . .?

Why don't you write a book containing all the tips that people have sent in to you. I am sure it would be very popular.
Jean Parker, Crestmead, Qld

That's your bloomin' lot, folks—Pete

Index

GARDENING

A U S T R A L I A

Pete's Mailbag is always full to bursting with hundreds of ideas, suggestions and experiments designed to make everyday gardening easier.

Here is Pete's own selection of heaps of the best of these clever tips from dedicated gardeners all over Australia.

Need a way to keep the birds off your seedlings; the sludge from your compost; the cats from your potplants, the dogs out of your snailbat? Want to know how to build a cheap and efficient soil sieve, garden kneeler, drip system, bulb storer, shadehouse or wasp trap?

Gardening Australia's viewers and readers have been through it all before and come up with all sorts of simple, and some complex, gadgets and gysmos to solve a myriad of gardening problems, making use of the most basic of raw materials—from coathangers to bedsprings, from orange bags to milk cartons, toilet rolls to corn cobs.

With no-nonsense explanations, simple diagrams and a very handy subject index, the friends of *Gardening Australia* give you the goods. This is their bloomin' book, so you can get down to it!